The Side Hustle Blueprint: Turning Ideas into Income

By Anthony Colasante

Table of Contents

Introduction

- The Power of the Side Hustle
- Why This Book?
- Who Is This Book For?

Chapter 1: Discovering Your Passion

- Identifying Your Interests and Skills
- Finding Marketable Ideas
- Turning Passions into Business Concepts

Chapter 2: Validating Your Idea

- Researching the Market
- Conducting Surveys and Feedback Loops
- Testing Your Idea with Minimal Investment

Chapter 3: Planning for Success

- Setting Clear Goals and Milestones

- Creating a Business Plan
- Budgeting and Financial Planning

Chapter 4: Building Your Brand

- Crafting a Unique Brand Identity
- Designing Logos, Websites, and Social Media Profiles
- Establishing a Strong Online Presence

Chapter 5: Setting Up Your Business

- Choosing the Right Business Structure
- Legal and Regulatory Considerations
- Setting Up Finances and Accounting

Chapter 6: Marketing Your Side Hustle

- Building a Marketing Strategy
- Leveraging Social Media and Content Marketing
- Networking and Collaborations

Chapter 7: Selling Your Products or Services

-

- Pricing Strategies and Models
- Sales Techniques and Best Practices

Handling Customer Service and Retention

Chapter 8: Scaling Up

- Automating Processes
- Hiring Help and Outsourcing

Expanding Product Lines or Services

Chapter 9: Managing Your Time

- Balancing a Full-Time Job and a Side Hustle
- Productivity Tips and Tools

Avoiding Burnout

Chapter 10: Overcoming Challenges

- Dealing with Failure and Setbacks
- Maintaining Motivation

Learning from Mistakes

Chapter 11: Real-Life Success Stories

- Case Studies of Successful Side Hustles
- Lessons Learned from Real Entrepreneurs

Chapter 12: Future-Proofing Your Business

- Adapting to Market Changes
- Continuous Learning and Development
- Preparing for Long-Term Success

Conclusion

- Reflecting on Your Journey
- Next Steps and Growth Opportunities
- Encouragement to Keep Going

Resources

- Templates, Tools, and Worksheets
- Recommended Reading
- Online Courses and Communities

Appendix

- Glossary of Terms
- Additional Case Studies and Examples

Introduction

The Power of the Side Hustle

In today's fast-paced world, the concept of a "side hustle" has evolved from a mere hobby to a powerful tool for financial freedom and personal fulfillment. Whether it's to supplement your income, explore a passion, or create a safety net, a side hustle offers a unique opportunity to take control of your financial destiny. It's more than just an extra source of cash; it's a way to turn your ideas into reality, build something meaningful, and, in some cases, create a full-time business from what started as a small venture.

A side hustle allows you to test the waters of entrepreneurship without the pressure of quitting your day job. It gives you the flexibility to experiment, learn, and grow at your own pace. You can start small, make mistakes, and adjust your course without the fear of financial ruin. And as your side hustle grows, so does your confidence and understanding of what it takes to run a successful business.

In this book, we will explore the incredible potential of side hustles, sharing practical advice and real-life examples to help you turn your passion project into a profitable side business. Whether you're dreaming of launching an online store, offering consulting services, or creating digital content, this guide will provide you with the tools and insights you need to get started and grow your venture.

Why This Book?

"From Idea to Reality: How to Start and Grow a Successful Side Hustle" was born out of a desire to help aspiring entrepreneurs navigate the often overwhelming process of starting and growing a side business. I know firsthand how daunting it can be to juggle a full-time job while trying to bring a new idea to life. The uncertainty, the time constraints, and the fear of failure can make the journey feel impossible. But with the right guidance and a clear roadmap, it doesn't have to be.

This book is designed to be a comprehensive resource, breaking down the process of launching a side hustle into manageable steps. Each chapter is filled with actionable advice, practical tips, and inspiring stories from individuals who have successfully transformed their side hustles into thriving businesses. Whether you're just starting out or looking to take your existing side hustle to the next level, this book will guide you every step of the way.

I've written this book to be your companion on this journey, providing you with the knowledge and motivation you need to succeed. My goal is to demystify the process, offering clear, straightforward advice that you can apply immediately. By the end of this book, you'll have a solid plan in place and the confidence to turn your ideas into a reality.

Who Is This Book For?

This book is for anyone who has ever dreamed of starting a side hustle but didn't know where to begin. Whether you're a full-time professional looking to supplement your income, a stay-at-home parent seeking to explore your passions, or a student eager to gain entrepreneurial experience, this guide is for you.

If you have an idea that you're passionate about, but you're unsure how to validate it, market it, or turn it into a profitable business, this book will provide the answers. Even if you're already running a side hustle and want to take it to the next level, you'll find valuable insights and strategies to help you grow and scale your business.

No matter your background or experience level, "From Idea to Reality" is designed to meet you where you are and help you achieve your entrepreneurial goals. This book is not just about making money—it's about building something you're proud of, something that aligns with your values and brings you fulfillment.

So, if you're ready to turn your idea into reality and embark on the exciting journey of entrepreneurship, let's get started. The world of side hustles is waiting for you, and with the right guidance, there's no limit to what you can achieve.

Chapter 1: Discovering Your Passion

The foundation of any successful side hustle is passion. When you're passionate about what you're doing, work doesn't feel like a burden—it becomes something you look forward to, even after a long day at your regular job. But how do you translate your interests and skills into a viable business idea? This chapter will guide you through the process of discovering what truly excites you and how to turn that passion into a profitable side hustle.

Identifying Your Interests and Skills

The first step in discovering your passion is to take a close look at your interests and skills. What activities make you lose track of time? What topics do you find yourself constantly drawn to? These are often clues to what you're truly passionate about.

Start by making a list of your hobbies, interests, and the things you enjoy doing in your free time. Don't limit yourself to what you think could be profitable—just focus on what you genuinely enjoy. Are you an avid photographer? Do you love writing? Perhaps you have a knack for DIY projects or enjoy helping others solve problems. No interest is too small or too niche; the goal is to identify what brings you joy.

Next, consider your skills and strengths. What are you good at? These can be technical skills, like coding or graphic design, or soft skills, like communication or organization. Think about the tasks you excel at in your current job or the activities that friends and family often ask you for help with. Your side hustle should ideally be at the intersection of what you love and what you're good at.

Once you have a list of your interests and skills, look for patterns or connections. For example, if you love photography and have strong social media skills, perhaps you could start a side hustle offering photography services and managing social media accounts for small businesses. The key is to find a way to combine your passions and skills into a business idea that excites you.

Finding Marketable Ideas

Now that you've identified your passions and skills, it's time to explore how they can be translated into a marketable business idea. The goal here is to find a niche where your interests align with market demand.

Start by researching your interests online. What are others doing in this space? Are there successful businesses that align with your passions? Look for gaps in the market—unmet needs or underserved audiences that you could target with your side hustle.

One effective way to find marketable ideas is to solve a problem you've encountered yourself. Think about challenges you've faced in your own life or in your work. Could your side hustle provide a solution? For example, if you've struggled to find affordable, high-quality graphic design services for your small business, perhaps there's an opportunity to offer those services to others.

Another approach is to tap into trends and emerging markets. Are there new technologies or shifts in consumer behavior that align with your interests? Staying ahead of trends can give you a competitive edge and help you create a side hustle that's in demand.

Don't be afraid to think outside the box. Sometimes the most successful side hustles are born from unconventional ideas. Consider how you can put a unique spin on your passions or combine them in unexpected ways. The more distinct your offering, the easier it will be to stand out in a crowded market.

Turning Passions into Business Concepts

Once you've identified a marketable idea, the next step is to refine it into a concrete business concept. This involves defining your target audience, understanding their needs, and determining how your side hustle will meet those needs.

Start by creating a profile of your ideal customer. Who are they? What are their pain points? How can your product or service improve their lives? The more specific you can be, the better. Understanding your target audience will help you tailor your offerings and marketing efforts to resonate with the right people.

Next, consider the value proposition of your side hustle. What makes your product or service unique? Why should customers choose you over competitors? Your value proposition should clearly communicate the benefits of your offering and why it's the best solution for your target audience.

At this stage, it's also important to think about how you'll deliver your product or service. Will it be an online business, a physical product, or a service-based side hustle? How will you reach your customers? Will you sell directly to consumers, partner with other businesses, or use online platforms to distribute your offering? Answering these questions will help you start to shape the logistics of your side hustle.

Finally, don't be afraid to start small. Your initial business concept doesn't have to be perfect or fully formed. The important thing is to take that first step and start testing your idea. You can always refine and adjust as you gain more experience and feedback from customers. Remember, many successful businesses started as simple side projects that evolved over time.

By the end of this chapter, you should have a clear understanding of your passions, a list of marketable ideas, and a solid business concept to start working on. Your side hustle journey begins with discovering what you love—and with the insights you've gained, you're now ready to take the next step toward turning your idea into reality.

Chapter 2: Validating Your Idea

Having a great idea is an essential first step, but the success of your side hustle depends on how well that idea resonates with your target market. Validation is the process of determining whether there's a demand for your product or service before you invest significant time and money into it. In this chapter, we'll explore how to research the market, gather feedback, and test your idea with minimal investment to ensure it has the potential to succeed.

Researching the Market

The first step in validating your idea is to thoroughly research the market. Understanding the landscape you're entering will help you identify opportunities, potential competitors, and the needs of your target audience. Market research is essential for determining whether your idea has the potential to thrive in the real world.

Identify Your Target Audience

Start by clearly defining your target audience. Who are they? What are their demographics, interests, and behaviors? Understanding your audience will guide your research and help you create a product or service that meets their needs. If you haven't already created a customer profile, now is the time to do so. This profile should include details such as age, gender, income level, location, and any other relevant characteristics that describe your ideal customer.

Analyze the Competition

Next, take a close look at your competitors. Who else is offering a similar product or service? How are they positioning themselves in the market? What are their strengths and weaknesses? Analyzing your competition will give you insights into what's already working in the market and where there may be gaps you can fill. Look at their pricing strategies, marketing tactics, and customer reviews to understand what customers appreciate and what they feel is lacking.

Assess Market Demand

Once you've identified your audience and competitors, assess the overall demand for your idea. Are there trends that suggest a growing interest in your niche? Use tools like Google Trends, keyword research, and social media analysis to gauge how often people are searching for or talking about products or services similar to yours. If you find that demand is strong and growing, it's a good sign that your idea has potential.

Explore Industry Reports and Publications

Industry reports, market studies, and publications can provide valuable data on market size, growth projections, and consumer behavior in your industry. These resources can help you understand the broader context in which your side hustle will operate and identify emerging trends or opportunities. Many reports are available for free or at a low cost through industry associations, research firms, or government agencies.

Conducting Surveys and Feedback Loops

Once you've done your initial market research, the next step in validation is to gather direct feedback from potential customers. Conducting surveys and setting up feedback loops will help you understand what your target audience thinks about your idea and whether they would actually pay for your product or service.

Create and Distribute Surveys

Surveys are a powerful tool for gathering quantitative and qualitative data from your target audience. They allow you to ask specific questions about their needs, preferences, and willingness to pay for your offering. When creating a survey, keep it short and focused to encourage participation. Ask open-ended questions to gather insights and closed-ended questions to quantify responses.

Distribute your survey through various channels, such as email, social media, and online communities where your target audience is active. Offer an incentive, like a discount or a small gift, to encourage people to participate. Be sure to analyze the results carefully, looking for patterns and common themes in the responses.

Set Up Feedback Loops

In addition to surveys, consider setting up ongoing feedback loops to continuously gather input from your audience. This could be as simple as inviting potential customers to join a mailing list where you regularly share updates and ask for feedback. You could also create a private Facebook group or Slack community where members can discuss your idea and provide suggestions.

Feedback loops are particularly useful as you refine your idea and start to develop prototypes or beta versions of your product. They allow you to test different aspects of your offering and make adjustments based on real-world input. Engaging with your audience early and often will not only help you validate your idea but also build a community of supporters who are invested in your success.

Testing Your Idea with Minimal Investment

One of the most effective ways to validate your side hustle idea is to test it in the real world with minimal investment. This approach allows you to gather valuable data and refine your concept without committing significant resources upfront. Here are some strategies to test your idea on a small scale:

Launch a Minimum Viable Product (MVP)

A Minimum Viable Product (MVP) is a simplified version of your product or service that includes only the essential features needed to solve the core problem for your customers. The goal of an MVP is to test your idea with real users, gather feedback, and make improvements based on their experiences.

For example, if your side hustle idea is an online course, you could start by offering a single lesson or module for free or at a low cost. This allows you to test the demand for your content, gather feedback, and refine your course before investing in a full-scale launch.

Offer a Pilot Program

Another way to test your idea is by offering a pilot program to a small group of customers. A pilot program is a limited, trial version of your product or service designed to gather feedback and prove the concept. This approach works well for service-based businesses, such as consulting, coaching, or freelance work.

To launch a pilot program, reach out to a select group of potential customers and offer them your service at a discounted rate or for free in exchange for their feedback. Use the insights you gather to refine your offering and prepare for a broader launch.

Pre-Sell Your Product or Service

Pre-selling is a strategy where you offer your product or service for sale before it's fully developed. This approach allows you to validate demand and generate revenue upfront, which can be reinvested into the development of your side hustle.

For example, if you're planning to launch a new product, you could create a landing page with detailed information about the product and offer it for pre-order. If you reach your pre-order goals, it's a strong indicator that there's demand for your idea. If not, you can reassess and make adjustments before moving forward.

Start with a Side Project

If your side hustle idea requires more time and resources to develop, consider starting with a related side project that allows you to test the waters. This could be a blog, YouTube channel, or social media account where you share content related to your idea and engage with your target audience. Over time, you can use the insights and audience you build through your side project to inform and validate your side hustle.

By testing your idea with minimal investment, you reduce the risk of failure and increase your chances of success. These small-scale tests provide valuable data and feedback, allowing you to refine your concept and build confidence in your side hustle before scaling up.

By the end of this chapter, you should have a clear understanding of how to validate your side hustle idea through market research, customer feedback, and real-world testing. Validation is a critical step in ensuring that your idea has the potential to succeed, and it will set the foundation for everything that comes next. With a validated idea in hand, you're now ready to move on to planning and building your side hustle.

Chapter 3: Planning for Success

Planning is the backbone of any successful side hustle. While passion and creativity are crucial, they must be coupled with a solid plan that guides your efforts and keeps you on track. In this chapter, we'll explore how to set clear goals and milestones, create a business plan, and develop a budget that will ensure your side hustle's financial health.

Setting Clear Goals and Milestones

One of the most important steps in turning your side hustle into a success is setting clear, achievable goals. Goals provide direction, motivation, and a way to measure progress. Without them, it's easy to lose focus or get discouraged when challenges arise.

Define Your Long-Term Vision

Start by defining your long-term vision for your side hustle. What do you want to achieve in the next year, five years, or even ten years? Your vision should be ambitious yet realistic, reflecting both your aspirations and the market realities. For example, your long-term vision might be to turn your side hustle into a full-time business, reach a specific revenue target, or become a leader in your niche.

Set SMART Goals

Once you have a clear vision, break it down into specific, measurable, achievable, relevant, and time-bound (SMART) goals. SMART goals provide a clear framework that helps you track progress and stay focused. For example, instead of setting a vague goal like "grow my business," a SMART goal would be "increase monthly revenue by 20% within the next six months by launching a new product line."

Establish Milestones

Milestones are smaller, intermediate steps that help you achieve your larger goals. They serve as checkpoints where you can assess your progress and make adjustments if needed. For example, if your goal is to increase revenue, milestones might include developing a marketing plan, launching a new product, or reaching a specific number of sales.

Create a timeline for your milestones, and be sure to celebrate each achievement. Recognizing your progress, even in small increments, will keep you motivated and committed to your side hustle.

Creating a Business Plan

A business plan is a roadmap that outlines the strategic direction of your side hustle. It provides clarity on your goals, target market, competitive landscape, and financial projections. Even if you're starting small, having a business plan in place will help you stay organized and focused.

Executive Summary

The executive summary is a brief overview of your business plan, summarizing the key points. It should include your side hustle's mission, goals, and what makes it unique. Although it's the first section of your business plan, it's often best to write it last, once you've fleshed out the details of your plan.

Business Description

In this section, describe your side hustle in detail. What products or services will you offer? What problem does your side hustle solve, and how does it add value to your customers? Include information about your business structure, such as whether you'll operate as a sole proprietor, partnership, or LLC.

Market Analysis

Conduct a thorough analysis of your target market and industry. This should include a detailed profile of your target audience, an overview of your competitors, and insights into market trends that could impact your side hustle. Understanding the market landscape is crucial for making informed decisions and identifying opportunities for growth.

Marketing and Sales Strategy

Outline your marketing and sales strategy, including how you plan to attract and retain customers. This might involve content marketing, social media, email campaigns, or partnerships. Be specific about the tactics you'll use and the channels you'll focus on. Additionally, define your sales process and any tools or platforms you'll use to manage customer relationships.

Operations Plan

The operations plan details how you'll run your side hustle on a day-to-day basis. This includes information about production, distribution, and the logistics of delivering your product or service to customers. If you're planning to hire help or outsource certain tasks, include that information here as well.

Financial Plan

Your financial plan should include projections for your side hustle's revenue, expenses, and profits. This is where you outline your budget, pricing strategy, and financial goals. Include a break-even analysis, which shows how much revenue you need to cover your costs, and cash flow projections to ensure you can manage your finances effectively.

Appendix

The appendix is an optional section where you can include additional information that supports your business plan. This might include market research data, product photos, or legal documents.

While creating a business plan may seem daunting, it's a valuable exercise that forces you to think critically about every aspect of your side hustle. It's also a living document that you can revisit and update as your business evolves.

Budgeting and Financial Planning

Financial planning is crucial for the long-term success of your side hustle. Without a clear understanding of your finances, it's easy to overspend, undercharge, or run into cash flow problems. A well-thought-out budget will help you manage your resources effectively and ensure your side hustle remains profitable.

Estimate Your Startup Costs

Start by estimating the initial costs required to get your side hustle off the ground. These might include costs for materials, equipment, website development, marketing, legal fees, and any other expenses necessary to launch. Be as detailed as possible, and don't forget to factor in unexpected costs that might arise.

Determine Your Pricing Strategy

Your pricing strategy will have a significant impact on your side hustle's profitability. Consider the costs of production, market demand, competitor pricing, and the value your product or service offers to customers. Make sure your prices cover your costs and provide a reasonable profit margin. If you're unsure where to start, consider testing different pricing models to see what resonates best with your customers.

Create a Monthly Budget

Once you've estimated your startup costs and determined your pricing, create a monthly budget to track your income and expenses. Your budget should include all recurring costs, such as materials, marketing, software subscriptions, and any fees associated with running your side hustle. Additionally, track your revenue to ensure you're meeting your financial goals.

Monitor Cash Flow

Cash flow is the lifeblood of any business. Even if your side hustle is profitable on paper, poor cash flow management can lead to financial difficulties. Keep a close eye on your cash flow by regularly reviewing your budget and financial statements. Make sure you have enough cash on hand to cover your expenses, especially during slower periods.

Plan for Taxes

As a side hustle owner, you'll need to set aside money for taxes. This includes self-employment taxes, income taxes, and any other applicable taxes depending on your business structure. It's wise to consult with a tax professional to ensure you're setting aside the correct amount and taking advantage of any deductions or credits available to you.

Build an Emergency Fund

An emergency fund is a financial safety net that can help you cover unexpected expenses or survive a temporary downturn in revenue. Aim to save at least three to six months' worth of expenses in your emergency fund. Having this cushion will give you peace of mind and allow you to take calculated risks without jeopardizing your financial stability.

By setting clear goals, creating a detailed business plan, and carefully managing your finances, you're laying the groundwork for a successful side hustle. These steps will help you stay organized, focused, and prepared for the challenges and opportunities that lie ahead. With a solid plan in place, you're now ready to move on to the exciting phase of building your brand and bringing your side hustle to life.

Chapter 4: Building Your Brand

Your brand is more than just a logo or a catchy slogan—it's the essence of your side hustle, the way you present yourself to the world, and the impression you leave on your customers. A strong brand identity sets you apart from the competition, builds trust with your audience, and creates a lasting connection with your customers. In this chapter, we'll explore how to craft a unique brand identity, design effective branding elements like logos and websites, and establish a strong online presence that will help your side hustle thrive.

Crafting a Unique Brand Identity

A brand identity is the combination of visual, verbal, and emotional elements that represent your side hustle. It's how your business looks, sounds, and feels to your customers. Crafting a unique brand identity is crucial for standing out in a crowded market and making a memorable impression.

Define Your Brand Values and Mission

The foundation of your brand identity lies in your values and mission. What does your side hustle stand for? What are the core principles that guide your business decisions? Your brand values should reflect what you believe in and what you want your business to represent. For example, if sustainability is important to you, that value should be woven into every aspect of your brand, from your product sourcing to your marketing messages.

Your brand mission, on the other hand, is a concise statement that defines the purpose of your side hustle. It should clearly articulate what you do, who you do it for, and why it matters. A strong mission statement will not only guide your brand identity but also resonate with your target audience, creating a deeper connection.

Identify Your Brand Personality

Every brand has a personality, which is the human-like characteristics that define how your brand interacts with the world. Is your brand fun and playful, or serious and professional? Is it bold and daring, or calm and nurturing? Defining your brand personality will help you create a consistent tone and style across all your branding elements.

To identify your brand personality, think about how you want your customers to perceive your side hustle. Consider the emotions you want to evoke and the type of relationship you want to build with your audience. Your brand personality should align with your target market and differentiate you from your competitors.

Develop Your Brand Voice

Your brand voice is the way you communicate with your audience, both in written and spoken form. It's an extension of your brand personality and should be consistent across all your marketing materials, from your website copy to your social media posts. A strong brand voice helps you connect with your audience on a deeper level and builds trust over time.

To develop your brand voice, start by considering how you want to sound to your customers. Do you want to be conversational and approachable, or authoritative and expert? Once you've defined your brand voice, create guidelines to ensure that everyone who writes or speaks on behalf of your side hustle maintains a consistent tone and style.

Create a Visual Identity

Your visual identity is the combination of visual elements that represent your brand, including your logo, color palette, typography, and imagery. These elements should work together to create a cohesive and recognizable look for your side hustle.

-

- **Logo:** Your logo is the centerpiece of your visual identity. It's the symbol that customers will associate with your brand, so it's important to create a logo that is memorable, versatile, and reflective of your brand values and personality. Consider working with a professional designer to create a logo that captures the essence of your side hustle.

- **Color Palette:** Colors have a powerful impact on emotions and perceptions, so choose a color palette that aligns with your brand personality and resonates with your target audience. For example, blue often conveys trust and professionalism, while yellow can evoke feelings of happiness and energy. Your color palette should be used consistently across all your branding materials.

- **Typography:** The fonts you choose for your brand play a key role in conveying your brand personality. Whether you opt for a clean, modern typeface or a more traditional, elegant font, make sure your typography is easy to read and aligns with your overall brand identity.

- **Imagery:** The images and graphics you use in your branding should reinforce your brand message and create a cohesive visual experience. Whether you use photographs, illustrations, or icons, make sure your imagery is high-quality and consistent with your brand's look and feel.

Designing Logos, Websites, and Social Media Profiles

Once you've established your brand identity, it's time to bring it to life through the design of key branding elements. These include your logo, website, and social media profiles—each of which plays a critical role in how your brand is perceived by customers.

Designing a Logo

Your logo is often the first thing people notice about your brand, so it's important to create a design that is both impactful and representative of your side hustle. When designing your logo, keep the following tips in mind:

- **Simplicity:** A simple logo is more likely to be remembered and recognized. Avoid overly complex designs and focus on creating a clean, straightforward symbol that conveys your brand essence.
- **Versatility:** Your logo should work well across various mediums and sizes, from business cards to billboards. Make sure it's scalable and looks good in both color and black-and-white formats.
- **Timelessness:** Aim for a logo that will stand the test of time. While it's tempting to follow design trends, a timeless logo will ensure your brand remains relevant for years to come.

If you're not a designer, consider hiring a professional or using an online logo design service. Investing in a well-designed logo is worth it, as it will be a central part of your brand identity.

Creating a Website

In today's digital world, a website is essential for establishing your online presence and reaching potential customers. Your website is often the first place people will go to learn more about your side hustle, so it's important to create a site that is professional, user-friendly, and reflective of your brand.

- **Homepage:** Your homepage is the face of your website, so make sure it clearly communicates what your side hustle is all about. Use your brand voice to engage visitors and guide them to the information they're looking for.

- **About Page:** The about page is where you can tell your brand's story and connect with your audience on a personal level. Share your mission, values, and the journey that led you to start your side hustle.

- **Product or Service Pages:** These pages should provide detailed information about your offerings, including features, benefits, pricing, and any relevant images or videos. Make sure your product or service pages are easy to navigate and designed to convert visitors into customers.

- **Contact Page:** Make it easy for potential customers to get in touch with you by including a contact page with your email address, phone number, and social media links. If applicable, include a contact form to streamline inquiries.

When designing your website, prioritize user experience (UX) and ensure that your site is mobile-friendly. A well-designed website not only reinforces your brand identity but also helps build credibility and trust with your audience.

Optimizing Social Media Profiles

Social media is a powerful tool for building your brand and connecting with your audience. Your social media profiles should be an extension of your brand identity, consistently reflecting your brand voice, visual identity, and values.

- **Profile Picture:** Use your logo as your profile picture to reinforce brand recognition across all platforms.

- **Bio:** Your bio should be a concise statement that communicates what your side hustle is all about. Use your brand voice to make it engaging and memorable, and include a link to your website.

- **Content:** The content you share on social media should align with your brand identity and provide value to your audience. Whether you're posting images, videos, or written content, make sure it's consistent with your brand's tone and style.

- **Engagement:** Social media is all about building relationships, so make sure you're engaging with your followers by responding to comments, answering questions, and participating in conversations. This will help you build a loyal community around your brand.

Choose the social media platforms that best align with your target audience and brand goals. It's better to focus on a few platforms and do them well than to spread yourself too thin across many.

Establishing a Strong Online Presence

In today's digital age, establishing a strong online presence is essential for the success of your side hustle. Your online presence encompasses your website, social media profiles, online reviews, and any other digital touchpoints where customers can interact with your brand.

Consistency is Key

Consistency is crucial when building an online presence. Make sure that your brand identity is reflected across all your digital channels, from your website and social media to your email marketing and online ads. This consistency not only reinforces your brand identity but also builds trust with your audience.

Content Marketing

Content marketing is a powerful strategy for establishing your brand as an authority in your niche and attracting potential customers. Consider creating a blog, YouTube channel, or podcast where you can share valuable content that aligns with your brand and resonates with your target audience. Whether it's how-to guides, industry insights, or behind-the-scenes looks at your side hustle, consistent, high-quality content can help you build an engaged audience and drive traffic to your website.

Search Engine Optimization (SEO)

Search Engine Optimization (SEO) is the process of optimizing your website and content to rank higher in search engine results, making it easier for potential customers to find you online. Effective SEO involves using relevant keywords, creating high-quality content, and ensuring your website is user-friendly and fast-loading. Investing in SEO can significantly boost your online visibility and drive organic traffic to your site.

Email Marketing

Email marketing is one of the most effective ways to build relationships with your audience and drive sales. Build an email list by offering valuable content or incentives, such as discounts or free resources, in exchange for subscribers' email addresses. Use your email marketing campaigns to share updates, promotions, and valuable content that aligns with your brand.

Online Reviews and Reputation Management

Online reviews can make or break your side hustle, so it's important to actively manage your online reputation. Encourage satisfied customers to leave positive reviews on platforms like Google, Yelp, or industry-specific review sites. If you receive negative feedback, respond promptly and professionally, addressing the issue and showing that you care about your customers' experiences.

Collaborations and Influencer Marketing

Collaborations with other brands or influencers can help you reach new audiences and build credibility. Look for opportunities to partner with businesses or individuals who align with your brand values and have a following that overlaps with your target market. Influencer marketing, where influencers promote your product or service to their audience, can be particularly effective for building brand awareness and trust.

By crafting a unique brand identity, designing effective branding elements, and establishing a strong online presence, you're setting your side hustle up for success. Your brand is the face of your business, and by investing time and effort into building it, you're creating a powerful tool that will help you attract customers, build loyalty, and stand out in a competitive market. With your brand in place, you're now ready to move on to marketing your side hustle and driving growth.

Chapter 5: Setting Up Your Business

Setting up your business properly from the start is crucial for ensuring that your side hustle operates smoothly and remains compliant with legal and regulatory requirements. In this chapter, we'll cover the key steps involved in choosing the right business structure, understanding legal and regulatory considerations, and setting up your finances and accounting systems.

Choosing the Right Business Structure

The business structure you choose will have significant implications for your side hustle, including how you pay taxes, your level of personal liability, and the amount of paperwork required. It's important to select a structure that aligns with your business goals, financial situation, and long-term plans. Here are the most common business structures to consider:

Sole Proprietorship

A sole proprietorship is the simplest and most common business structure for side hustles. It's easy to set up and gives you full control over your business. However, as a sole proprietor, there's no legal distinction between you and your business, meaning you're personally liable for any debts or legal issues. This structure is best suited for low-risk businesses that don't require significant investment.

Partnership

If you're starting your side hustle with one or more partners, a partnership might be the right choice. In a partnership, each partner contributes to the business and shares in the profits and losses. There are two main types of partnerships: general partnerships, where all partners share liability and management responsibilities, and limited partnerships, where some partners have limited liability but less control over the business.

Partnerships are relatively easy to set up but require a clear partnership agreement to avoid disputes.

Limited Liability Company (LLC)

An LLC is a popular choice for side hustles because it offers the liability protection of a corporation with the tax flexibility of a sole proprietorship or partnership. As an LLC owner, your personal assets are protected from business liabilities, meaning you're not personally responsible for the company's debts or legal issues. LLCs are relatively easy to set up and maintain, making them a good option for side hustlers who want a balance of protection and simplicity.

Corporation

A corporation is a more complex business structure that provides the highest level of liability protection. It's a separate legal entity from its owners, meaning the corporation itself can enter into contracts, sue or be sued, and own assets. There are two main types of corporations: C corporations, which are subject to double taxation (once on profits and again on dividends), and S corporations, which allow profits to pass through to shareholders without being taxed at the corporate level. Corporations require more paperwork and compliance, making them better suited for larger or more complex businesses.

Choosing the Right Structure

When deciding on a business structure, consider factors such as the level of risk in your industry, your long-term business goals, and how much time and money you're willing to invest in compliance and paperwork. If you're unsure which structure is best for your side hustle, it's a good idea to consult with a business attorney or accountant who can provide guidance based on your specific situation.

Legal and Regulatory Considerations

Once you've chosen your business structure, it's important to ensure that your side hustle complies with all legal and regulatory requirements. This will help you avoid fines, lawsuits, and other legal issues that could derail your business.

Registering Your Business Name

If you're operating under a name other than your own, you'll need to register your business name with the appropriate government authority. This process, known as filing a "Doing Business As" (DBA) name, ensures that your business name is unique and legally protected. The specific requirements for registering a DBA vary by state or country, so be sure to check with your local government.

Obtaining Licenses and Permits

Depending on your industry and location, you may need to obtain certain licenses or permits to operate your side hustle legally. Common examples include business licenses, sales tax permits, health department permits (for food-related businesses), and professional licenses (for services like accounting or real estate). Failure to obtain the necessary permits can result in fines or the shutdown of your business, so it's important to research the requirements in your area.

Understanding Tax Obligations

As a business owner, you'll need to comply with various tax obligations, including income tax, self-employment tax, and sales tax. The specific taxes you'll need to pay depend on your business structure and location.

- **Income Tax:** You'll need to report your side hustle's income on your personal tax return if you're a sole proprietor, partner, or LLC owner. Corporations file separate tax returns.

- **Self-Employment Tax:** If you're self-employed, you're responsible for paying both the employer and employee portions of Social Security and Medicare taxes. This is typically calculated as a percentage of your net earnings from your side hustle.
- **Sales Tax:** If you sell products or services that are subject to sales tax, you'll need to collect sales tax from your customers and remit it to the appropriate tax authority. The rules for sales tax vary by state, so be sure to understand your obligations.

Drafting Contracts and Agreements

Contracts and agreements are essential for protecting your side hustle from legal disputes. Whether you're working with clients, partners, or suppliers, having clear, written agreements in place ensures that everyone understands their rights and responsibilities.

- **Client Contracts:** If you provide services, create a standard contract that outlines the scope of work, payment terms, deadlines, and any other relevant details. This protects both you and your clients by setting clear expectations from the start.
- **Partnership Agreements:** If you're entering into a partnership, draft a partnership agreement that outlines each partner's contributions, responsibilities, and how profits and losses will be shared. This helps prevent misunderstandings and conflicts down the road.
- **Supplier Agreements:** If you're working with suppliers or vendors, have them sign an agreement that outlines the terms of your relationship, including pricing, delivery

schedules, and quality standards. This ensures that both parties are on the same page and reduces the risk of disputes.

Consider working with an attorney to draft these documents, especially if your side hustle involves complex legal issues or high-value transactions.

Setting Up Finances and Accounting

Proper financial management is critical for the success of your side hustle. Setting up your finances and accounting systems correctly from the start will help you stay organized, track your business's performance, and ensure that you meet your tax obligations.

Opening a Business Bank Account

One of the first steps in setting up your finances is to open a separate business bank account. Keeping your personal and business finances separate makes it easier to track your income and expenses, and it's essential for maintaining accurate financial records. A business bank account also simplifies tax preparation and helps establish your side hustle as a legitimate business in the eyes of the IRS and other authorities.

Setting Up Accounting Software

Accounting software is an invaluable tool for managing your side hustle's finances. It allows you to track income and expenses, generate invoices, manage payroll (if applicable), and produce financial reports. There are many accounting software options available, ranging from simple solutions like QuickBooks or Wave for small businesses to more robust systems like Xero or FreshBooks for growing businesses.

When choosing accounting software, look for features that match your business needs, such as integration with your bank account, automatic expense categorization, and the ability to generate financial statements. Many software options also offer cloud-based access, allowing you to manage your finances from anywhere.

Tracking Income and Expenses

Accurate tracking of income and expenses is essential for understanding your side hustle's financial health and preparing for tax season. Make it a habit to record every transaction, whether it's income from a sale or an expense for supplies. Categorize your expenses to see where your money is going and identify areas where you can cut costs.

Some key expense categories to track include:

- **Cost of Goods Sold (COGS):** The direct costs of producing your products, such as materials and manufacturing.
- **Operating Expenses:** The ongoing costs of running your business, such as rent, utilities, marketing, and software subscriptions.
- **Travel and Meals:** If you travel for business or meet with clients, track these expenses to deduct them from your taxes.
- **Professional Services:** Expenses for legal, accounting, or consulting services.

By keeping detailed records, you'll have a clear picture of your profitability and be better prepared to make informed financial decisions.

Budgeting and Cash Flow Management

Creating a budget for your side hustle helps you plan for expenses, manage cash flow, and set financial goals. Your budget should include both fixed costs (such as rent or software subscriptions) and variable costs (such as materials or marketing).

Cash flow management is crucial for ensuring that your side hustle has enough money to cover expenses and invest in growth. Keep a close eye on your cash flow by regularly reviewing your income and expenses. If you notice that cash is tight, look for ways to increase revenue, reduce expenses, or negotiate better payment terms with suppliers.

Tax Preparation and Filing

As a side hustle owner, you're responsible for filing your taxes accurately and on time. This includes paying estimated quarterly taxes if you expect to owe more than a certain amount in federal taxes. Keep detailed records of your income, expenses, and deductions to make tax preparation easier.

Consider working with a tax professional, especially if your side hustle involves complex tax issues, such as multiple income streams or international clients. A tax professional can help you maximize deductions, comply with tax laws, and avoid costly mistakes.

Building an Emergency Fund

An emergency fund is a financial cushion that can help you weather unexpected expenses or downturns in revenue. Aim to save at least three to six months' worth of operating expenses in your emergency fund. This provides peace of mind and allows you to focus on growing your side hustle without worrying about financial setbacks.

By choosing the right business structure, understanding legal and regulatory considerations, and setting up your finances and accounting, you're laying the foundation for a successful and sustainable side hustle. These steps may seem daunting, but they're essential for protecting your business, managing your money effectively, and ensuring long-term growth. With your business now properly set up, you're ready to focus on marketing your side hustle and bringing in customers.

Chapter 6: Marketing Your Side Hustle

Marketing is the engine that drives your side hustle, turning your business ideas into profits by attracting customers and building brand awareness. A well-executed marketing strategy not only brings in revenue but also helps establish your brand's identity and reputation. In this chapter, we'll cover how to build a comprehensive marketing strategy, leverage social media and content marketing, and use networking and collaborations to grow your side hustle.

Building a Marketing Strategy

Your marketing strategy is the blueprint for how you will reach your target audience and achieve your business goals. It should be tailored to your unique side hustle, taking into account your brand identity, target market, and available resources.

Define Your Target Audience

The first step in building a marketing strategy is to clearly define your target audience. Who are your ideal customers? What are their demographics, interests, and pain points? Understanding your audience allows you to create marketing messages that resonate with them and choose the right channels to reach them.

Create detailed customer personas that represent different segments of your audience. These personas should include information such as age, gender, occupation, income level, and hobbies. The more specific you can be, the better you'll be able to tailor your marketing efforts to meet their needs.

Set Marketing Goals

Next, set specific, measurable marketing goals that align with your overall business objectives. These goals should be SMART (Specific, Measurable, Achievable, Relevant, and Time-bound).

For example, a goal might be to increase website traffic by 25% over the next three months or to acquire 100 new email subscribers within the next month.

Your marketing goals will guide your strategy and help you measure the effectiveness of your efforts. Break down your goals into actionable steps and assign deadlines to keep your strategy on track.

Choose Your Marketing Channels

There are numerous marketing channels available, but not all will be suitable for your side hustle. Choose the channels that are most likely to reach your target audience and align with your brand identity. Some common marketing channels include:

- **Social Media:** Platforms like Instagram, Facebook, Twitter, and LinkedIn allow you to connect with your audience, share content, and promote your products or services.
- **Content Marketing:** Blogging, video creation, and podcasting help you provide value to your audience, establish authority in your niche, and drive traffic to your website.
- **Email Marketing:** Building an email list allows you to communicate directly with your audience, promote offers, and nurture customer relationships.
- **Paid Advertising:** Pay-per-click (PPC) ads, social media ads, and display ads can help you reach a larger audience quickly, though they require a budget.
- **SEO:** Search Engine Optimization helps your website rank higher in search engine results, driving organic traffic to your site.

- **Events and Workshops:** Hosting or participating in events, webinars, or workshops can help you connect with your audience in person or online, building stronger relationships and trust.

Consider your budget, resources, and the preferences of your target audience when selecting your marketing channels. It's often better to focus on a few key channels and do them well rather than spreading yourself too thin across many.

Craft Your Brand Message

Your brand message is the core idea or promise that you want to communicate to your audience. It should be consistent across all your marketing efforts and reflect your brand values, mission, and personality. A strong brand message resonates with your audience and sets you apart from competitors.

To craft your brand message, consider the following questions:

- What value does your side hustle provide to customers?
- What problem does it solve, and how does it improve their lives?
- What makes your brand unique in the market?

Once you've defined your brand message, incorporate it into your marketing materials, website copy, social media posts, and any other communication with your audience.

Develop a Content Calendar

A content calendar is a valuable tool for planning and organizing your marketing activities. It helps you stay consistent with your marketing efforts and ensures that you're delivering the right content to your audience at the right time.

When creating a content calendar, consider important dates, such as product launches, holidays, or industry events, and plan your marketing activities around them. Include details such as content topics, formats (e.g., blog posts, videos, emails), publication dates, and responsible team members. Having a well-structured content calendar will help you stay organized and maintain momentum in your marketing efforts.

Leveraging Social Media and Content Marketing

Social media and content marketing are powerful tools for building brand awareness, engaging with your audience, and driving traffic to your website. When used effectively, these channels can significantly contribute to the growth of your side hustle.

Social Media Marketing

Social media platforms offer a direct line of communication with your audience, allowing you to share your brand message, promote your products or services, and build relationships with potential customers. Here's how to leverage social media for your side hustle:

- **Choose the Right Platforms:** Focus on the platforms where your target audience is most active. For example, Instagram and Pinterest are ideal for visually-driven brands, while LinkedIn is better suited for B2B businesses.
- **Create Engaging Content:** Share a mix of content that provides value to your audience, such as educational posts, behind-the-scenes looks, user-generated content, and promotional offers. Use a consistent tone and style that reflects your brand personality.

- **Build a Community:** Engage with your followers by responding to comments, answering questions, and participating in conversations. Building a community around your brand fosters loyalty and encourages word-of-mouth marketing.
- **Utilize Hashtags and Keywords:** Use relevant hashtags and keywords to increase the visibility of your posts and reach a wider audience. Research popular hashtags in your niche and incorporate them into your posts.
- **Analyze and Adjust:** Regularly review your social media analytics to see what's working and what's not. Use insights from your data to refine your strategy and improve your results over time.

Content Marketing

Content marketing involves creating and sharing valuable content that attracts and engages your target audience. By providing useful information, you can establish yourself as an authority in your niche, build trust with your audience, and drive traffic to your website.

- **Blogging:** A blog is a great way to share your expertise, answer common questions, and provide solutions to your audience's problems. Consistently publishing high-quality blog posts can improve your SEO and position your brand as a go-to resource in your industry.
- **Video Content:** Videos are highly engaging and can be used to demonstrate your products, share customer testimonials, or provide how-to guides. Platforms like YouTube, Instagram, and TikTok are ideal for sharing video content and reaching a broader audience.

- **Podcasting:** If your audience prefers audio content, consider starting a podcast where you discuss topics related to your niche, interview industry experts, or share your insights. Podcasts are a great way to connect with your audience on a deeper level and build brand loyalty.
- **E-books and Guides:** Offering free e-books, guides, or whitepapers can help you capture leads and build your email list. These resources should provide valuable information that solves a specific problem or answers a key question for your audience.
- **Email Newsletters:** Regular email newsletters allow you to stay in touch with your audience, share updates, and promote your products or services. Use your email list to nurture leads, provide exclusive offers, and drive repeat business.

The key to successful content marketing is consistency. Develop a content strategy that aligns with your brand message and audience needs, and commit to delivering high-quality content on a regular basis.

Networking and Collaborations

Networking and collaborations are effective ways to expand your reach, build relationships, and gain credibility in your industry. By connecting with other businesses, influencers, and professionals, you can tap into new audiences and create mutually beneficial opportunities.

Attend Industry Events

Industry events, such as conferences, trade shows, and workshops, provide valuable opportunities to network with like-minded professionals and potential customers. Attend events relevant to your niche to learn about industry trends, connect with influencers, and promote your side hustle.

When attending events, be prepared with business cards, an elevator pitch, and a clear understanding of what you want to achieve. Whether it's building relationships, finding collaborators, or gaining new clients, having a clear goal will help you make the most of your networking opportunities.

Join Online Communities

Online communities, such as forums, social media groups, and industry-specific platforms, are great places to connect with your target audience and other professionals in your niche. Join communities where your ideal customers are active, and contribute by sharing valuable insights, answering questions, and participating in discussions.

Building a presence in online communities can help you establish yourself as an authority in your field and create opportunities for collaborations, partnerships, and customer referrals.

Collaborate with Influencers

Influencer marketing involves partnering with individuals who have a strong following in your niche to promote your products or services. Collaborating with influencers can help you reach a larger audience, build credibility, and drive sales.

When choosing influencers to collaborate with, look for those who align with your brand values and have an engaged following. Influencer collaborations can take many forms, including sponsored posts, product reviews, giveaways, or joint content creation. Be sure to establish clear terms for the collaboration, including compensation, deliverables, and timelines.

Partner with Complementary Businesses

Collaborating with complementary businesses can help you reach new customers and create win-win opportunities. For example, if you sell handmade candles, you could partner with a local spa or wellness brand to create a bundled offer or cross-promote each other's products.

Partnerships can take many forms, including co-hosting events, running joint promotions, or creating co-branded products. Look for businesses that share your target audience but aren't direct competitors, and explore ways to work together that benefit both parties.

Leverage Customer Referrals

Word-of-mouth marketing is one of the most powerful forms of promotion. Encourage your satisfied customers to refer friends, family, or colleagues to your side hustle by offering referral incentives, such as discounts, freebies, or exclusive offers.

You can also create a formal referral program where customers earn rewards for bringing in new business. Make it easy for customers to refer others by providing them with shareable content, referral links, or social media posts.

By building a solid marketing strategy, leveraging social media and content marketing, and utilizing networking and collaborations, you'll be well-equipped to grow your side hustle and attract a steady stream of customers. Marketing is an ongoing process, so be prepared to continuously refine your approach, stay up-to-date with industry trends, and adapt to changes in the market. With the right marketing efforts in place, you're on the path to long-term success and growth for your side hustle.

Chapter 7: Selling Your Products or Services

Selling your products or services effectively is crucial to the success of your side hustle. It's not just about setting a price and hoping for the best; it's about understanding your market, employing the right sales techniques, and building strong relationships with your customers. In this chapter, we'll explore various pricing strategies and models, share effective sales techniques, and discuss how to handle customer service and retention to ensure long-term success.

Pricing Strategies and Models

Pricing your products or services correctly is a delicate balance between covering your costs, maximizing profits, and offering value to your customers. The right pricing strategy can make all the difference in attracting customers and ensuring your side hustle is sustainable.

Understand Your Costs

Before setting your prices, you need to have a clear understanding of your costs. This includes both direct costs (such as materials, production, and shipping) and indirect costs (such as marketing, overhead, and taxes). Make sure to account for all expenses involved in bringing your product or service to market.

Once you've calculated your total costs, you can determine your break-even point—the minimum price at which you need to sell your product or service to cover your costs. This will serve as the baseline for your pricing strategy.

Consider Your Value Proposition

Your pricing should reflect the value your product or service offers to customers. Consider what makes your offering unique and why customers would choose you over competitors. If you offer superior quality, exceptional customer service, or a unique feature, you may be able to charge a premium price.

On the other hand, if you're entering a competitive market and your primary advantage is affordability, you may need to adopt a more aggressive pricing strategy to attract price-sensitive customers. Always align your pricing with your value proposition to ensure you're appealing to the right audience.

Explore Different Pricing Models

There are several pricing models you can choose from, depending on your business type and goals. Here are some common options:

- **Cost-Plus Pricing:** This model involves adding a markup to your total costs to determine the selling price. For example, if your product costs $10 to produce and you want a 50% markup, you would set the price at $15. Cost-plus pricing is straightforward but may not always reflect the value perceived by customers.
- **Value-Based Pricing:** Value-based pricing focuses on the perceived value of your product or service to the customer rather than just the cost of production. This model is often used for premium or niche products where customers are willing to pay more for the perceived benefits.
- **Competitive Pricing:** Competitive pricing involves setting your prices based on what your competitors are charging. This model is useful in highly competitive markets where price is a key factor in customer decision-making. You can choose to match, undercut, or exceed competitor prices depending on your positioning.
- **Dynamic Pricing:** Dynamic pricing adjusts prices based on real-time demand and market conditions. This model is commonly used in industries like travel and hospitality, but

- it can also be applied to e-commerce and other sectors. Dynamic pricing requires sophisticated data analysis but can help maximize profits during peak demand periods.

- **Freemium Model:** The freemium model offers a basic version of your product or service for free, with the option to upgrade to a premium version with additional features. This model is popular in software and digital services and can be effective for building a large user base and converting free users into paying customers.

- **Subscription Pricing:** Subscription pricing involves charging customers a recurring fee (monthly, quarterly, or annually) for access to your product or service. This model provides a steady revenue stream and works well for businesses offering ongoing value, such as memberships, digital content, or software-as-a-service (SaaS).

Test and Adjust Your Pricing

Pricing is not a one-time decision. It's important to test different pricing strategies and models to see what works best for your side hustle. Consider running A/B tests or offering promotional pricing to gauge customer response. Monitor your sales data and customer feedback closely, and be prepared to adjust your pricing as needed to optimize profitability and customer satisfaction.

Sales Techniques and Best Practices

Effective sales techniques are essential for converting prospects into paying customers and driving revenue growth. Whether you're selling online, in person, or over the phone, the following sales practices can help you close more deals and build lasting customer relationships.

Understand Your Customer's Needs

Successful selling starts with understanding your customer's needs, pain points, and motivations. Before making a sales pitch, take the time to listen to your prospects and ask questions that uncover their specific challenges and goals. The more you know about your customer, the better you can tailor your offering to meet their needs.

For example, if you're selling a software solution, ask the prospect about their current workflow, the challenges they're facing, and what they hope to achieve with your product. Use this information to highlight the features and benefits that are most relevant to their situation.

Build Rapport and Trust

People are more likely to buy from businesses they trust, so building rapport with your prospects is key to closing sales. Be genuine, approachable, and professional in all your interactions. Show that you care about their success and are invested in finding the best solution for them.

Building trust also involves being transparent about your product or service. Don't make promises you can't keep or oversell the benefits. Instead, focus on providing accurate information and setting realistic expectations. If your product isn't the right fit for a prospect, it's better to be honest than to push for a sale that may lead to dissatisfaction later on.

Highlight Benefits, Not Just Features

When presenting your product or service, focus on the benefits it provides rather than just listing features. Customers are more interested in how your offering will solve their problems or improve their lives than in technical specifications.

For example, instead of saying, "Our software has a built-in CRM," emphasize the benefit: "Our software helps you streamline customer management, so you can close deals faster and keep track of all your interactions in one place." By highlighting the benefits, you make it easier for customers to see the value in your offering.

Use Social Proof

Social proof is a powerful sales tool that leverages the influence of others to build credibility and trust. This can take the form of customer testimonials, case studies, reviews, or endorsements from industry experts.

Share success stories from satisfied customers who have benefited from your product or service. If possible, include specific results, such as increased sales, time savings, or improved efficiency. Social proof reassures prospects that others have had positive experiences with your side hustle, making them more likely to buy.

Create a Sense of Urgency

Creating a sense of urgency can motivate prospects to take action and make a purchase. Limited-time offers, scarcity (e.g., "only 5 spots left"), and special promotions are all effective ways to encourage customers to buy now rather than later.

However, be careful not to overuse urgency tactics, as they can lose their effectiveness if customers feel pressured or manipulated. The goal is to nudge prospects towards a decision, not to rush them into a purchase they might regret.

Overcome Objections

Objections are a natural part of the sales process, and being prepared to address them can make the difference between a lost sale and a successful one. Common objections include concerns about price, timing, or whether your product is the right fit.

Listen carefully to your prospect's objections and respond with empathy. Acknowledge their concerns, provide additional information or reassurance, and offer solutions that address their specific worries. For example, if a prospect is concerned about the price, you could highlight the long-term value and return on investment (ROI) they'll receive.

Close the Sale

The final step in the sales process is closing the sale. This involves asking for the customer's commitment and finalizing the transaction. There are several techniques you can use to close a sale, depending on the situation:

- **Assumptive Close:** Assume the customer is ready to buy and proceed with the next steps. For example, "Great, let's get you set up. Would you like to start with the monthly or annual plan?"
- **Alternative Close:** Offer the customer a choice between two options, both of which lead to a sale. For example, "Would you prefer the standard package or the premium package?"
- **Urgency Close:** Use urgency to encourage the customer to act quickly. For example, "This offer is only available until the end of the week. Can I secure your spot today?"

Regardless of the technique you use, the key is to be confident and clear in your approach. After you've made your pitch, don't be afraid to ask for the sale directly. If the customer is ready, guide them through the purchase process smoothly and efficiently.

Handling Customer Service and Retention

Customer service and retention are critical components of a successful side hustle. It's not enough to simply make a sale; you need to ensure that your customers are satisfied, supported, and willing to come back for more. By focusing on customer service and retention, you can build a loyal customer base that drives repeat business and word-of-mouth referrals.

Provide Exceptional Customer Service

Exceptional customer service starts with being responsive, helpful, and attentive to your customers' needs. Whether it's answering questions, resolving issues, or providing guidance, make sure your customers feel valued and supported throughout their experience with your side hustle.

- **Be Responsive:** Respond to customer inquiries and concerns promptly. Whether it's via email, phone, or social media, aim to reply within 24 hours or sooner if possible.
- **Listen Actively:** When interacting with customers, listen to their concerns and feedback without interrupting. Show empathy and understanding, and make an effort to address their needs.
- **Go the Extra Mile:** Look for opportunities to exceed customer expectations, whether it's by offering personalized recommendations, following up after a purchase, or including a handwritten thank-you note with their order.

Handle Complaints and Issues Gracefully

No matter how well you run your side hustle, there will inevitably be times when things go wrong. Whether it's a product defect, shipping delay, or miscommunication, how you handle customer complaints can make or break your reputation.

-

- **Acknowledge the Issue:** When a customer raises a complaint, acknowledge the issue and apologize for any inconvenience caused. Even if the problem wasn't your fault, taking responsibility shows that you care about the customer's experience.
- **Offer a Solution:** Provide a solution that addresses the customer's concerns, whether it's a refund, replacement, or other forms of compensation. Make sure the customer is satisfied with the resolution before closing the conversation.
- **Follow Up:** After resolving the issue, follow up with the customer to ensure everything is now satisfactory. This extra step shows that you're committed to their satisfaction and can help rebuild trust.

Encourage Repeat Business

Customer retention is about turning one-time buyers into loyal, repeat customers. It's often more cost-effective to retain existing customers than to acquire new ones, so focus on building long-term relationships.

- **Create Loyalty Programs:** Offer loyalty programs that reward repeat customers with discounts, special offers, or exclusive access to new products. This incentivizes customers to continue doing business with you.
- **Stay in Touch:** Regularly communicate with your customers through email newsletters, social media, or personalized messages. Keep them informed about new products, promotions, and any updates to your side hustle.

Ask for Feedback: Encourage customers to provide feedback on their experience, and use their input to improve your products, services, and processes. Showing that you value their opinions can strengthen the relationship and foster loyalty.

Leverage Customer Referrals

Happy customers are often willing to refer others to your side hustle, so make it easy for them to do so. Create a referral program that rewards customers for bringing in new business, whether through discounts, freebies, or other incentives.

Provide your customers with shareable content, referral links, or social media posts they can use to spread the word. Word-of-mouth marketing is one of the most effective ways to grow your side hustle, as referrals come with a built-in level of trust.

By implementing the right pricing strategies, employing effective sales techniques, and prioritizing customer service and retention, you'll be well on your way to building a successful and sustainable side hustle. Selling is not just about closing deals; it's about creating value for your customers and building relationships that lead to repeat business and long-term growth. With these strategies in place, you're poised to not only attract customers but also turn them into loyal advocates for your brand.

Chapter 8: Scaling Up

As your side hustle grows, you'll reach a point where you need to scale up to meet increasing demand, optimize efficiency, and unlock new revenue opportunities. Scaling up involves automating processes, hiring help, outsourcing tasks, and expanding your product lines or services. In this chapter, we'll explore how to scale your side hustle strategically and sustainably.

Automating Processes

One of the most effective ways to scale your side hustle is by automating repetitive tasks and processes. Automation can save you time, reduce errors, and allow you to focus on higher-value activities, such as product development, marketing, and customer relationships.

Identify Tasks to Automate

Start by identifying the tasks that are repetitive, time-consuming, or prone to human error. These might include:

- **Order Processing:** Automating order processing ensures that orders are received, fulfilled, and tracked with minimal manual intervention. E-commerce platforms like Shopify or WooCommerce offer built-in automation tools to streamline this process.
- **Email Marketing:** Use email marketing automation tools like Mailchimp, ConvertKit, or HubSpot to schedule and send emails, segment your audience, and trigger automated campaigns based on customer behavior.
- **Social Media Posting:** Automate your social media posts using tools like Buffer, Hootsuite, or Later. These

platforms allow you to schedule posts in advance, manage multiple accounts, and analyze engagement metrics.

- **Invoicing and Payments:** Automate invoicing and payment collection using tools like QuickBooks, FreshBooks, or Stripe. These platforms can generate invoices, send payment reminders, and track payments automatically.

- **Customer Support:** Implement chatbots or automated email responses to handle common customer inquiries. Tools like Intercom, Drift, or Zendesk can help you provide instant support without the need for manual intervention.

Choose the Right Tools

Once you've identified the tasks you want to automate, research and choose the right tools that fit your side hustle's needs and budget. Many automation tools offer free trials or tiered pricing plans, so you can start small and upgrade as your business grows.

When selecting tools, consider factors such as ease of use, integration with your existing systems, scalability, and customer support. The goal is to implement automation that simplifies your operations without adding complexity.

Monitor and Optimize Automation

Automation isn't a set-it-and-forget-it solution. Regularly monitor your automated processes to ensure they're working as intended and delivering the desired results. Track key performance indicators (KPIs) such as time saved, error reduction, and customer satisfaction.

Be prepared to make adjustments as needed. For example, you may need to tweak your email marketing automation based on open rates and click-through rates, or refine your social media scheduling based on engagement metrics. Continuous optimization ensures that your automation efforts contribute to your side hustle's growth.

Hiring Help and Outsourcing

As your side hustle expands, you may find that you can no longer manage all aspects of the business on your own. Hiring help or outsourcing tasks can free up your time, bring in specialized expertise, and allow you to focus on strategic growth initiatives.

Determine What to Delegate

Start by identifying the tasks that are consuming too much of your time or require skills that you may not have. Common areas to delegate or outsource include:

- **Administrative Tasks:** Data entry, appointment scheduling, email management, and other routine tasks can be delegated to a virtual assistant (VA).
- **Customer Service:** Outsource customer support to a VA or a customer service agency to handle inquiries, returns, and other customer interactions.
- **Content Creation:** Hire freelance writers, designers, or videographers to create blog posts, social media content, videos, or marketing materials.
- **Website Maintenance:** If you're not technically inclined, consider outsourcing website updates, security, and maintenance to a web developer or IT professional.
-

Accounting and Bookkeeping: An accountant or bookkeeper can manage your finances, prepare financial statements, and ensure compliance with tax regulations.

Hire the Right People

When hiring help, it's essential to find the right people who align with your side hustle's values, goals, and work style. Start by clearly defining the roles and responsibilities you need to fill. Create detailed job descriptions that outline the skills, experience, and qualifications required for each position.

For small tasks or specialized projects, consider hiring freelancers or contractors through platforms like Upwork, Fiverr, or Toptal. For more ongoing or integral roles, you may want to hire part-time or full-time employees. Use job boards, social media, and your professional network to find candidates.

During the hiring process, take the time to interview candidates, review their portfolios or references, and assess their fit with your company culture. It's better to invest time upfront in finding the right person than to rush the hiring process and risk costly mistakes.

Outsource Strategically

Outsourcing allows you to tap into expertise and resources that you may not have in-house, without the overhead of hiring full-time staff. When outsourcing, look for reputable agencies or freelancers with a proven track record in the area you need help with.

Clearly define the scope of work, deliverables, and timelines in a written contract. Maintain open communication with your outsourced partners to ensure that they understand your expectations and are aligned with your goals.

Outsourcing is particularly useful for tasks that require specialized skills, such as digital marketing, SEO, graphic design, or software development. It can also be a cost-effective way to scale up operations without committing to long-term hires.

Build a Strong Team Culture

Whether you're hiring employees or working with freelancers, building a strong team culture is essential for collaboration and productivity. Clearly communicate your side hustle's mission, values, and goals to your team. Foster an environment of trust, respect, and open communication.

Encourage regular check-ins, team meetings, and feedback sessions to keep everyone aligned and motivated. Recognize and reward your team's contributions, and create opportunities for professional growth and development. A strong team culture not only enhances performance but also contributes to employee retention and satisfaction.

Expanding Product Lines or Services

Scaling up often involves expanding your product lines or services to reach new markets, increase revenue, and diversify your offerings. Introducing new products or services can help you attract more customers, enhance your brand's value, and reduce reliance on a single revenue stream.

Identify Expansion Opportunities

Start by analyzing your existing products or services to identify potential areas for expansion. Consider the following approaches:

- **Product Variations:** Offer new variations of your existing products, such as different sizes, colors, or flavors. For example, if you sell candles, you could introduce new scents or packaging options.

- **Complementary Products:** Introduce products that complement your existing offerings and enhance the customer experience. For example, if you sell fitness equipment, you could add workout apparel or accessories to your product line.
- **Bundling:** Create product bundles or packages that offer customers a better value while increasing your average order value. For example, you could bundle a product with complementary items or offer a subscription box with curated products.
- **New Services:** If your side hustle is service-based, consider adding new services that address additional customer needs. For example, if you offer web design services, you could expand into SEO, content creation, or social media management.
- **Digital Products:** Digital products, such as e-books, courses, templates, or software, can be a scalable way to expand your offerings without the need for physical inventory. Digital products can also generate passive income and reach a global audience.

Test and Validate New Offerings

Before fully committing to a new product line or service, it's important to test and validate the idea to ensure there's demand. Start by conducting market research to understand customer preferences, pricing expectations, and potential competitors.

Consider launching a pilot program or limited-time offer to gauge customer interest and gather feedback. Use this information to refine your offering and make any necessary adjustments before a full-scale launch.

Testing and validation reduce the risk of investing time and resources into a product or service that may not resonate with your audience. It also allows you to make data-driven decisions and optimize your chances of success.

Plan for Production and Fulfillment

Scaling up your product line or services requires careful planning for production and fulfillment. Ensure that you have the capacity to produce and deliver your new offerings without compromising quality or customer satisfaction.

If you're expanding a physical product line, assess your supply chain, inventory management, and logistics to ensure you can meet demand. Consider working with new suppliers, increasing production runs, or partnering with a fulfillment center to handle shipping and warehousing.

For service-based expansions, consider the resources and skills needed to deliver the new services effectively. This may involve hiring additional staff, investing in training, or acquiring new tools and software.

Market Your New Offerings

Once you've developed and tested your new products or services, create a marketing plan to promote them to your existing customers and attract new ones. Leverage your existing channels, such as email marketing, social media, and your website, to announce the launch and generate excitement.

Consider offering special promotions, discounts, or limited-time offers to incentivize early purchases and gather customer reviews. Highlight the benefits and value of your new offerings, and use customer testimonials or case studies to build credibility.

If you're entering a new market or targeting a different audience, adjust your marketing strategy to align with their preferences and behaviors. This may involve exploring new marketing channels, creating targeted campaigns, or partnering with influencers in your niche.

Monitor and Optimize

As you scale up your side hustle by expanding your product lines or services, it's important to continuously monitor performance and optimize your approach. Track key metrics such as sales, customer feedback, profitability, and market trends.

Be prepared to make adjustments based on the data you collect. This may involve discontinuing underperforming products, tweaking pricing or packaging, or refining your marketing strategy. Scaling up is an iterative process, and staying agile will help you navigate challenges and capitalize on opportunities.

Scaling up your side hustle is an exciting phase of growth that requires careful planning, strategic decision-making, and a focus on efficiency. By automating processes, hiring help, outsourcing tasks, and expanding your product lines or services, you can take your business to the next level and achieve sustainable growth. With the right strategies in place, your side hustle can evolve into a thriving enterprise that continues to deliver value to customers and generate lasting success.

Chapter 9: Managing Your Time

Managing your time effectively is one of the most critical skills for side hustle success, especially if you're balancing it with a full-time job. With the right strategies, you can maximize productivity, maintain a healthy work-life balance, and avoid burnout. In this chapter, we'll explore how to balance your full-time job and side hustle, offer productivity tips and tools, and discuss ways to prevent burnout.

Balancing a Full-Time Job and a Side Hustle

Juggling a full-time job and a side hustle can be challenging, but it's achievable with careful planning and discipline. The key is to prioritize your time, set realistic expectations, and maintain a healthy work-life balance.

Set Clear Boundaries

One of the first steps in balancing a full-time job and a side hustle is to set clear boundaries between the two. Determine when and where you will work on your side hustle, and stick to that schedule as much as possible. This might mean dedicating specific hours before or after your day job, or setting aside weekends for side hustle activities.

It's important to communicate these boundaries with your employer, if necessary, to ensure that your side hustle doesn't interfere with your job performance. Similarly, communicate your schedule with family and friends to manage their expectations and gain their support.

Prioritize Your Tasks

With limited time available, it's essential to prioritize your tasks and focus on what will have the most significant impact on your side hustle's growth. Use the 80/20 rule (Pareto Principle) to identify the 20% of tasks that will generate 80% of the results. Prioritize these high-impact activities, such as marketing, sales, and product development, and minimize time spent on less critical tasks.

Create a daily or weekly to-do list that outlines your most important tasks. Break larger tasks into smaller, manageable steps, and tackle them one at a time. By prioritizing effectively, you can make steady progress on your side hustle without feeling overwhelmed.

Leverage Time Blocking

Time blocking is a productivity technique where you allocate specific blocks of time for different tasks throughout your day. This method helps you stay focused, minimize distractions, and ensure that you're dedicating enough time to both your full-time job and side hustle.

Start by identifying your peak productivity hours—when you're most alert and focused. Use these hours for tasks that require deep concentration, such as strategic planning, content creation, or product development. Reserve less demanding tasks, such as responding to emails or scheduling social media posts, for times when your energy levels are lower.

By planning your day in blocks, you can make the most of your time and reduce the risk of tasks spilling over into other areas of your life.

Stay Flexible

While it's important to have a schedule, it's equally important to stay flexible and adapt to unexpected changes. Life happens, and there will be times when your full-time job demands more of your attention, or personal obligations arise. When this happens, don't be too hard on yourself—adjust your schedule as needed and pick up where you left off when you can.

Flexibility also means being open to reevaluating your side hustle's priorities as it grows. What worked for you in the early stages may not be as effective as your business expands. Regularly assess your time management strategies and make adjustments to align with your evolving goals and responsibilities.

Productivity Tips and Tools

Maximizing your productivity is essential when you're managing both a full-time job and a side hustle. By using the right tools and techniques, you can work more efficiently, stay organized, and accomplish more in less time.

Use a Task Management System

A task management system helps you keep track of your to-do lists, deadlines, and progress. Whether you prefer digital tools or traditional planners, having a system in place ensures that nothing falls through the cracks.

Popular task management tools include:

- **Trello:** A visual project management tool that uses boards, lists, and cards to help you organize tasks and projects. Trello is great for tracking progress, setting deadlines, and collaborating with team members.
- **Asana:** A robust task management platform that allows you to create tasks, set priorities, assign them to team members, and track progress. Asana is ideal for managing both individual and team projects.
- **Todoist:** A simple yet powerful to-do list app that helps you organize tasks, set due dates, and prioritize your workload. Todoist is perfect for managing daily tasks and personal projects.
-

Notion: A versatile all-in-one workspace that combines notes, tasks, databases, and calendars. Notion is highly customizable and can be tailored to fit your unique workflow.

Implement the Pomodoro Technique

The Pomodoro Technique is a time management method that involves working in short, focused intervals (typically 25 minutes) followed by a short break. After four intervals, take a longer break. This technique helps maintain concentration, reduce fatigue, and improve productivity.

To implement the Pomodoro Technique:

1. Choose a task to work on.
2. Set a timer for 25 minutes (one Pomodoro).
3. Work on the task until the timer goes off.
4. Take a 5-minute break.
5. Repeat the process, taking a longer break (15-30 minutes) after every four Pomodoros.

You can use tools like the **Pomodone** app or a simple kitchen timer to track your intervals. The Pomodoro Technique is particularly effective for tasks that require intense focus and can help you maintain productivity throughout the day.

Automate Repetitive Tasks

As discussed in Chapter 8, automation is a powerful way to increase productivity by reducing the time spent on repetitive tasks. Identify tasks that can be automated, such as social media scheduling, email marketing, or invoicing, and use tools to streamline these processes.

For example, you can use **Zapier** to create automated workflows that connect different apps and services, saving you time on tasks like data entry or customer follow-ups. Automation allows you to focus on higher-value activities that contribute directly to your side hustle's growth.

Minimize Distractions

Distractions are a major productivity killer, especially when you're trying to balance multiple responsibilities. To minimize distractions:

- **Create a dedicated workspace:** Set up a specific area where you work on your side hustle, free from distractions like TV or household chores. If possible, choose a quiet space with minimal interruptions.
- **Turn off notifications:** Silence notifications on your phone, computer, and other devices while you're working. Consider using **Focus mode** on your phone or apps like **Freedom** to block distracting websites and apps.
- **Set boundaries:** Let family and friends know when you're working on your side hustle, and ask them to respect your time. Use noise-cancelling headphones or background music to block out external noise.
- **Limit multitasking:** Focus on one task at a time to improve efficiency and reduce errors. Multitasking can decrease productivity and increase stress, so try to complete one task before moving on to the next.

Use Time-Tracking Tools

Time-tracking tools can help you understand how you're spending your time and identify areas for improvement. By tracking your work hours, you can analyze your productivity patterns, set realistic goals, and ensure that you're allocating enough time to both your full-time job and side hustle.

Popular time-tracking tools include:

- **Toggl:** A simple time-tracking app that allows you to track time spent on tasks, projects, and clients. Toggl provides detailed reports that help you analyze your productivity and optimize your workflow.
- **RescueTime:** A tool that tracks how you spend your time on your computer and mobile devices. RescueTime provides insights into your habits, helps you identify distractions, and suggests ways to improve focus.
- **Clockify:** A free time-tracking tool that allows you to log hours, set timers, and generate reports. Clockify is great for freelancers and entrepreneurs who need to track billable hours or manage multiple projects.

By regularly tracking your time, you can make data-driven decisions to improve your productivity and work-life balance.

Avoiding Burnout

Balancing a full-time job and a side hustle can be demanding, and it's easy to fall into the trap of overworking and burning out. Burnout not only affects your productivity but also your mental and physical health. To avoid burnout, it's essential to take care of yourself, set realistic expectations, and maintain a healthy work-life balance.

Recognize the Signs of Burnout

Burnout can manifest in various ways, including physical, emotional, and mental exhaustion. Common signs of burnout include:

-

- **Chronic fatigue:** Feeling constantly tired, even after a good night's sleep.
- **Decreased motivation:** Losing interest or enthusiasm for your side hustle or job.
- **Irritability:** Feeling easily frustrated or annoyed by minor inconveniences.
- **Difficulty concentrating:** Struggling to focus on tasks or make decisions.
- **Physical symptoms:** Experiencing headaches, muscle tension, or digestive issues.

If you notice any of these signs, it's important to take action to prevent burnout from worsening.

Set Realistic Expectations

One of the main causes of burnout is setting unrealistic expectations for yourself. While it's natural to want to achieve your goals quickly, pushing yourself too hard can lead to exhaustion and frustration.

Be honest with yourself about what you can realistically accomplish given your time and resources. Set achievable goals, and break them down into smaller, manageable steps. Remember that building a successful side hustle takes time, and it's okay to pace yourself.

Take Regular Breaks

Taking regular breaks is essential for maintaining energy and focus. Make sure to schedule short breaks throughout your workday, as well as longer breaks for meals and relaxation. Step away from your desk, stretch, go for a walk, or do something enjoyable to recharge.

In addition to daily breaks, make time for regular vacations or days off to disconnect from work and recharge your batteries. Taking time off can improve your productivity and creativity in the long run.

Practice Self-Care

Self-care is crucial for preventing burnout and maintaining your overall well-being. Make time for activities that nourish your mind, body, and soul, such as:

- **Exercise:** Regular physical activity can reduce stress, improve mood, and boost energy levels. Find a form of exercise that you enjoy, whether it's walking, yoga, cycling, or dancing.
- **Healthy Eating:** Fuel your body with nutritious foods that provide sustained energy and support mental clarity. Avoid relying on caffeine or sugar to get through the day.
- **Sleep:** Prioritize getting enough sleep each night to support your cognitive function, mood, and physical health. Aim for 7-9 hours of quality sleep and establish a consistent bedtime routine.
- **Mindfulness:** Practice mindfulness techniques such as meditation, deep breathing, or journaling to manage stress and stay present in the moment.
- **Hobbies:** Engage in hobbies or activities that bring you joy and relaxation, whether it's reading, painting, gardening, or spending time with loved ones.

Learn to Say No

One of the most important skills in avoiding burnout is learning to say no. As your side hustle grows, you may be tempted to take on every opportunity that comes your way. However, overcommitting can lead to overwhelm and burnout.

Set boundaries around your time and energy, and be selective about the projects or tasks you take on. Prioritize the activities that align with your goals and values, and don't be afraid to decline opportunities that don't serve your best interests.

Seek Support

Balancing a full-time job and a side hustle can be isolating, so it's important to seek support from others. Talk to friends, family, or mentors about your challenges, and don't hesitate to ask for help when needed.

Consider joining a community of like-minded entrepreneurs or side hustlers who understand the unique challenges you face. Online forums, social media groups, and local meetups can provide valuable support, advice, and camaraderie.

If you're struggling with stress or burnout, consider seeking professional support from a therapist or counselor. They can provide tools and strategies to help you manage stress, set boundaries, and prioritize your well-being.

Managing your time effectively is crucial for balancing a full-time job and a side hustle while maintaining your health and well-being. By setting clear boundaries, prioritizing tasks, leveraging productivity tools, and practicing self-care, you can achieve your goals without sacrificing your quality of life. Avoiding burnout is key to sustaining your side hustle in the long term and ensuring that you continue to enjoy the journey. With the right strategies in place, you can manage your time effectively, stay productive, and build a successful side hustle while maintaining a healthy work-life balance.

Chapter 10: Overcoming Challenges

Every side hustle journey comes with its own set of challenges, from dealing with failure and setbacks to maintaining motivation and learning from mistakes. How you respond to these challenges will ultimately determine your success. In this chapter, we'll explore strategies for overcoming obstacles, staying motivated during difficult times, and turning your mistakes into valuable lessons.

Dealing with Failure and Setbacks

Failure and setbacks are inevitable in any entrepreneurial journey. Whether it's a product that doesn't sell, a marketing campaign that falls flat, or a financial loss, these experiences can be disheartening. However, how you deal with these setbacks will shape your resilience and ability to succeed in the long run.

Embrace Failure as a Learning Opportunity

Instead of viewing failure as a negative outcome, try to see it as a valuable learning experience. Each setback provides an opportunity to gain insights, refine your approach, and improve your side hustle. Ask yourself what went wrong, why it happened, and what you can do differently in the future.

For example, if a product launch didn't go as planned, analyze the reasons behind it. Was it a lack of market research, insufficient marketing, or a misalignment with customer needs? Use these insights to adjust your strategy and make more informed decisions going forward.

Reframe Your Mindset

Adopting a growth mindset is crucial for overcoming challenges. A growth mindset is the belief that your abilities and intelligence can be developed through hard work, learning, and perseverance.

Instead of seeing failure as a reflection of your abilities, view it as an opportunity to grow and evolve.

When faced with a setback, remind yourself that every successful entrepreneur has encountered failures along the way. The key is to keep moving forward, learn from your experiences, and apply those lessons to future endeavors.

Take Action to Recover

After experiencing a setback, it's important to take proactive steps to recover and move forward. Start by assessing the situation objectively and identifying the most pressing issues. Create a plan to address these challenges, whether it involves adjusting your strategy, seeking additional resources, or pivoting to a new approach.

For example, if you're struggling with cash flow, consider cutting unnecessary expenses, renegotiating payment terms with suppliers, or seeking alternative revenue streams. Taking action not only helps you regain control but also restores your confidence and momentum.

Seek Support and Advice

You don't have to navigate challenges alone. Reach out to mentors, peers, or fellow entrepreneurs for support and advice. Sharing your experiences with others who have faced similar challenges can provide valuable insights and reassurance.

If you're facing a particularly difficult setback, consider seeking professional advice from a business coach, financial advisor, or consultant. They can offer objective perspectives, help you develop a recovery plan, and guide you through the decision-making process.

Maintaining Motivation

Staying motivated is essential for the long-term success of your side hustle. However, maintaining motivation can be challenging, especially during periods of slow progress, setbacks, or when balancing multiple responsibilities. Here are some strategies to help you stay motivated and keep moving forward.

Reconnect with Your "Why"

One of the most powerful ways to reignite your motivation is to reconnect with your original purpose or "why." Why did you start your side hustle in the first place? What are your long-term goals, and how does your side hustle align with your values and passions?

Take some time to reflect on your motivations and remind yourself of the positive impact your side hustle can have on your life and the lives of others. Whether it's achieving financial independence, pursuing a passion, or creating a legacy, keeping your "why" in mind can provide the motivation you need to keep going.

Set Short-Term Goals and Celebrate Progress

While long-term goals are important, setting short-term, achievable goals can help you stay motivated on a daily basis. Break down your larger goals into smaller milestones that you can work towards each week or month. Achieving these smaller goals provides a sense of accomplishment and keeps you moving in the right direction.

Celebrate your progress, no matter how small. Whether it's reaching a sales target, launching a new product, or completing a challenging task, acknowledging your achievements can boost your confidence and motivation. Consider rewarding yourself with something meaningful, like a day off, a special treat, or a small gift.

Create a Routine

Establishing a consistent routine can help you stay motivated and productive, even on days when you don't feel like working. A routine provides structure, reduces decision fatigue, and helps you develop positive habits that contribute to your side hustle's success.

Start by creating a daily or weekly schedule that outlines when you'll work on your side hustle and what tasks you'll focus on. Stick to your routine as much as possible, but also allow for flexibility to accommodate changes or unexpected events.

Visualize Success

Visualization is a powerful technique that can help you stay motivated by mentally picturing your future success. Take a few minutes each day to visualize yourself achieving your goals, whether it's launching a successful product, reaching a financial milestone, or receiving positive feedback from customers.

By imagining your success, you can create a sense of excitement and anticipation that drives you to take action. Visualization can also help you overcome self-doubt and reinforce your belief in your ability to succeed.

Surround Yourself with Positivity

Your environment plays a significant role in your motivation and mindset. Surround yourself with positive influences, such as supportive friends, family members, or fellow entrepreneurs who encourage and uplift you.

Consider joining a community or mastermind group of like-minded individuals who share your goals and values. Being part of a supportive community can provide motivation, accountability, and inspiration, especially during challenging times.

Take Breaks and Rest

Burnout can quickly drain your motivation, so it's important to take regular breaks and prioritize rest. Allow yourself time to recharge, both mentally and physically. Taking time off to relax, engage in hobbies, or spend time with loved ones can help you return to your side hustle with renewed energy and focus.

Remember that rest is not a sign of weakness or laziness—it's an essential part of maintaining long-term motivation and productivity. By taking care of yourself, you'll be better equipped to handle challenges and stay committed to your goals.

Learning from Mistakes

Mistakes are an inevitable part of the entrepreneurial journey, but they also provide valuable opportunities for growth and improvement. By learning from your mistakes, you can refine your approach, avoid repeating errors, and build a stronger, more resilient side hustle.

Acknowledge and Analyze Your Mistakes

The first step in learning from mistakes is to acknowledge them openly and without judgment. Avoid the temptation to ignore or downplay your mistakes—instead, view them as important learning experiences.

Take the time to analyze what went wrong and why. Ask yourself questions such as:

- What specific actions or decisions led to the mistake?
- Were there any warning signs or red flags that were overlooked?
- How did the mistake impact your side hustle, customers, or team?

By understanding the root causes of your mistakes, you can gain valuable insights that will help you make better decisions in the future.

Develop a Plan to Correct and Prevent Mistakes

Once you've identified the causes of a mistake, create a plan to correct it and prevent it from happening again. This may involve changing processes, improving communication, or seeking additional training or resources.

For example, if you made a mistake in financial management, consider implementing better budgeting tools, hiring a bookkeeper, or taking a course on financial literacy. If the mistake involved a misunderstanding with a client, work on improving your communication skills and setting clearer expectations.

Taking proactive steps to address mistakes shows that you're committed to continuous improvement and learning from your experiences.

Share Your Lessons with Others

Sharing your mistakes and the lessons you've learned with others can be a valuable way to reinforce your own learning and help others avoid similar pitfalls. Whether it's through blogging, social media, or speaking at events, being open about your challenges and how you overcame them can inspire and educate others in your community.

Additionally, seeking feedback from others who have faced similar challenges can provide new perspectives and ideas for how to move forward. Learning from the experiences of others can help you avoid common mistakes and accelerate your growth.

Embrace a Growth Mindset

A growth mindset is essential for turning mistakes into opportunities for improvement. Instead of viewing mistakes as failures, see them as part of the learning process. Embrace the idea that your skills and abilities can be developed over time, and that each mistake brings you one step closer to success.

Cultivate resilience by focusing on the progress you've made and the lessons you've learned, rather than dwelling on setbacks. By maintaining a positive and growth-oriented mindset, you'll be better equipped to navigate challenges and achieve your long-term goals.

Reflect and Adjust Regularly

Learning from mistakes is an ongoing process that requires regular reflection and adjustment. Set aside time to review your side hustle's performance, assess what's working and what's not, and make necessary changes.

Consider keeping a journal or log where you document your experiences, challenges, and lessons learned. This practice can help you track your progress, identify patterns, and stay accountable to your goals.

By consistently reflecting on your experiences and making adjustments, you can continuously improve your side hustle and increase your chances of long-term success.

Overcoming challenges is a fundamental part of building a successful side hustle. By dealing with failure and setbacks constructively, maintaining motivation during difficult times, and learning from your mistakes, you can develop the resilience and skills needed to thrive as an entrepreneur. Challenges are not obstacles to be feared, but opportunities to grow, learn, and become stronger. With the right mindset and strategies, you can overcome any challenge that comes your way and continue moving forward on your entrepreneurial journey.

Chapter 11: Real-Life Success Stories

Inspiration often comes from seeing how others have navigated the challenges and triumphs of building a side hustle. Real-life success stories provide valuable insights into what works, what doesn't, and the persistence required to turn a passion project into a thriving business. In this chapter, we'll explore case studies of successful side hustles and the lessons learned from real entrepreneurs who have walked the path before you.

Case Studies of Successful Side Hustles

Case Study 1: The Handmade Candle Business

Background: Sarah, a full-time marketing professional, had a passion for creating handmade candles. What started as a hobby, making candles for friends and family, quickly turned into a side hustle when she realized there was a growing market for high-quality, artisanal candles. With limited resources and time, Sarah decided to test the waters by selling her candles at local markets and online through Etsy.

Challenges: Sarah faced several challenges in the early stages, including competition from established brands, finding cost-effective suppliers, and managing her time between her full-time job and her growing side hustle. Additionally, scaling production to meet increasing demand without compromising quality was a significant hurdle.

Strategies:

- **Market Research:** Sarah conducted thorough market research to identify her target audience—individuals who valued eco-friendly, luxury candles. She positioned her brand to stand out by focusing on sustainable ingredients and unique, hand-poured designs.

- **Leverage Social Media:** Sarah used Instagram to showcase her candles, build a following, and engage with customers. She posted regularly, shared behind-the-scenes content, and collaborated with influencers to expand her reach.

- **Automate and Outsource:** To manage her time more effectively, Sarah automated parts of her business, such as social media scheduling and order processing. She also outsourced packaging and shipping to a fulfillment service, allowing her to focus on production and marketing.

Results: Within two years, Sarah's candle business grew from a small side project to a six-figure business. She was able to leave her full-time job and focus on her side hustle full-time. Her candles are now sold in boutique stores nationwide, and she has expanded her product line to include diffusers and home fragrance products.

Lessons Learned:

- **Niche Market Focus:** By identifying a specific niche and catering to it with high-quality products, Sarah was able to differentiate her brand and build a loyal customer base.

- **Consistency:** Regular posting on social media and engaging with her audience helped Sarah build brand awareness and trust, leading to increased sales and word-of-mouth referrals.

- **Outsourcing:** Recognizing the importance of her time, Sarah strategically outsourced tasks that were not her core strengths, allowing her to scale her business effectively.

Case Study 2: The Online Fitness Coach

Background: David was a personal trainer with a full-time job at a local gym. He noticed a growing demand for online fitness coaching, particularly from busy professionals who couldn't make it to the gym regularly. Seeing an opportunity, David decided to start an online fitness coaching side hustle, offering personalized workout plans and virtual training sessions.

Challenges: David's main challenges were building an online presence, acquiring clients in a crowded market, and managing his time between his day job and his side hustle. Additionally, transitioning from in-person training to virtual coaching required a new set of skills, particularly in digital marketing and technology.

Strategies:

- **Leverage Existing Networks:** David started by offering free training sessions to his existing clients and asking for testimonials and referrals. This helped him build credibility and attract his first online clients.

- **Content Marketing:** To reach a broader audience, David started a fitness blog and YouTube channel where he shared workout tips, nutrition advice, and success stories. This content attracted potential clients and positioned him as an expert in the online fitness space.

- **Online Platforms:** David used platforms like Instagram and LinkedIn to promote his services, share client transformations, and engage with his audience. He also joined online fitness communities to connect with potential clients and share his expertise.

Results: David's side hustle quickly gained traction, and within a year, he was generating more income from online coaching than from his full-time job. He eventually transitioned to running his online fitness business full-time, allowing him to work with clients globally and achieve a work-life balance that suited him.

Lessons Learned:

- **Leverage Existing Relationships:** David's initial success came from tapping into his existing network of clients and leveraging their testimonials and referrals to build credibility.
- **Content is King:** By consistently creating valuable content, David was able to attract and convert leads into paying clients. His blog and YouTube channel became key drivers of traffic and customer acquisition.
- **Adaptability:** David's willingness to learn new skills, such as digital marketing and video production, allowed him to transition from in-person training to a successful online business.

Case Study 3: The Subscription Box for Book Lovers

Background: Emily, a full-time teacher with a passion for reading, noticed that many book lovers were looking for curated book recommendations and related merchandise. She decided to launch a subscription box service that delivered a new book and book-themed goodies to subscribers each month. Emily started her side hustle with a small budget and a lot of enthusiasm.

Challenges: Emily faced challenges in sourcing quality products, managing inventory, and marketing her subscription service in a competitive space. Additionally, she needed to balance the demands of her teaching job with the growing responsibilities of running a business.

Strategies:

- **Pre-Launch Marketing:** Before launching, Emily built an email list by offering a free book-themed quiz and early-bird discounts. This helped her gauge interest and create buzz around her subscription box.
- **Partnerships:** Emily partnered with indie authors and local artisans to source unique items for her boxes. These partnerships allowed her to offer exclusive content and products, setting her box apart from competitors.
- **Customer Feedback:** Emily actively sought feedback from her subscribers to refine her offerings and improve customer satisfaction. She used surveys and social media polls to understand her audience's preferences and adapt her service accordingly.

Results: Within the first six months, Emily's subscription box service gained a steady subscriber base, and her business began to grow through word-of-mouth and positive reviews. She expanded her offerings to include themed boxes, gift subscriptions, and special editions. Her side hustle eventually became a profitable full-time business, allowing her to combine her love of teaching with her passion for reading by offering book-related educational content.

Lessons Learned:

- **Pre-Launch Preparation:** Building an email list and generating interest before launch helped Emily start her

business with a ready customer base, reducing the risk and uncertainty.
-
- **Unique Value Proposition:** By partnering with authors and artisans, Emily was able to offer a unique and curated experience that resonated with her target audience.
-

Customer-Centric Approach: Emily's commitment to listening to her customers and adapting her service based on feedback played a crucial role in her success.

Lessons Learned from Real Entrepreneurs

The experiences of these entrepreneurs highlight several key lessons that can be applied to your own side hustle journey:

1. Start Small and Test the Waters Many successful side hustles begin as small, low-risk ventures. Testing your idea on a small scale allows you to validate your concept, gather feedback, and make improvements before investing significant resources. Whether it's selling at local markets, offering free services, or running a pilot program, starting small helps you refine your offering and build confidence.

2. Leverage Your Existing Network Your existing network of friends, family, colleagues, and customers can be a valuable resource for getting your side hustle off the ground. Use these connections to gather initial feedback, secure your first customers, and build credibility. Word-of-mouth referrals and testimonials can be powerful tools for growing your business.

3. Focus on Your Niche Successful side hustles often focus on a specific niche, allowing you to stand out in a crowded market. By catering to a targeted audience with specialized needs, you can create a unique value proposition that differentiates your brand. Understanding your niche and tailoring your products, services, and marketing efforts to meet their needs is crucial for building a loyal customer base.

4. Be Willing to Learn and Adapt The entrepreneurial journey is filled with learning opportunities. Be open to acquiring new skills, whether it's digital marketing, content creation, or financial management. Embrace challenges as chances to grow, and be willing to pivot or adjust your strategy as needed. Flexibility and adaptability are key to navigating the ups and downs of running a side hustle.

5. Invest in Building Relationships Building strong relationships with customers, partners, and your community is essential for long-term success. Focus on providing exceptional customer service, engaging with your audience, and creating meaningful connections. Collaborations, partnerships, and customer loyalty can drive growth and open new opportunities for your side hustle.

6. Consistency is Key Consistency in your efforts, whether it's in marketing, customer service, or product quality, is crucial for building trust and credibility. Regularly engaging with your audience, delivering on your promises, and maintaining high standards will help you establish a strong reputation and foster repeat business.

7. Persistence Pays Off All entrepreneurs face setbacks, but those who persevere through challenges are more likely to succeed. Persistence, resilience, and a positive mindset are essential for overcoming obstacles and achieving your goals. Remember that success rarely happens overnight—it's the result of consistent effort, learning, and determination.

The real-life success stories of these entrepreneurs demonstrate that with the right mindset, strategies, and perseverance, it's possible to turn a side hustle into a thriving business. By learning from their experiences and applying the lessons they've shared, you can navigate the challenges of entrepreneurship and move closer to achieving your own side hustle dreams. Success is within reach for those who are willing to take risks, learn from failures, and keep pushing forward, no matter the obstacles.

Chapter 12: Future-Proofing Your Business

As your side hustle grows, it's crucial to think long-term and ensure that your business can adapt to changes in the market, technology, and consumer behavior. Future-proofing your business involves staying agile, continuously learning, and preparing for sustainable success. In this final chapter, we'll explore how to adapt to market changes, commit to continuous learning and development, and set your business up for long-term success.

Adapting to Market Changes

The business landscape is constantly evolving, with new trends, technologies, and consumer preferences emerging all the time. To ensure your side hustle remains relevant and competitive, you must be proactive in adapting to these changes.

Stay Informed About Industry Trends

Keeping up with industry trends is essential for staying ahead of the curve. Regularly read industry publications, blogs, and reports to stay informed about the latest developments in your niche. Follow thought leaders, attend webinars, and participate in industry conferences to gain insights and network with other professionals.

Set aside time each month to review industry news and assess how emerging trends might impact your side hustle. For example, if you're in the e-commerce space, stay informed about advancements in AI, changes in consumer behavior, or new marketing techniques. By staying informed, you can identify opportunities to innovate and adapt your business strategy accordingly.

Monitor Competitors

Competitor analysis is an ongoing process that can provide valuable insights into market shifts and customer preferences. Regularly review your competitors' products, services, marketing strategies, and customer feedback to understand what's working for them and where they might be vulnerable.

Use tools like Google Alerts, SEMrush, or Ahrefs to track competitor activity and analyze their online presence. Pay attention to how competitors are responding to market changes and consider how you can differentiate your side hustle or improve your offerings in response.

Be Willing to Pivot

In some cases, adapting to market changes may require a more significant pivot in your business model, product line, or target audience. A successful pivot involves making strategic changes to align your side hustle with new opportunities or address emerging challenges.

For example, during the COVID-19 pandemic, many businesses pivoted to online models, offering virtual services, curbside pickups, or e-commerce options to meet changing consumer needs. If you notice a shift in demand or encounter unforeseen challenges, be open to rethinking your approach and making the necessary adjustments to stay relevant.

Diversify Revenue Streams

Relying on a single product, service, or revenue stream can make your side hustle vulnerable to market changes. Diversifying your offerings can help you mitigate risk and create multiple sources of income.

Consider expanding your product line, offering complementary services, or exploring new markets to diversify your revenue streams. For example, if you sell physical products, you could introduce digital products, subscription services, or consulting services to create additional income opportunities. Diversification helps ensure that your business remains resilient in the face of market fluctuations.

Invest in Technology

Technology plays a critical role in the future-proofing of your business. Investing in the right tools and platforms can help you streamline operations, improve customer experiences, and stay competitive in a rapidly changing landscape.

Stay informed about technological advancements relevant to your industry, such as automation, artificial intelligence, data analytics, or digital marketing tools. Consider adopting new technologies that can enhance your efficiency, reduce costs, or provide valuable insights into customer behavior.

For example, implementing a customer relationship management (CRM) system can help you better manage customer interactions and data, while adopting an e-commerce platform with AI-driven recommendations can improve sales and customer satisfaction. Embracing technology allows you to stay agile and respond quickly to changing market conditions.

Continuous Learning and Development

In an ever-evolving business environment, continuous learning and development are essential for staying ahead and driving long-term success. Committing to ongoing education and skill development ensures that you and your team remain competitive and capable of adapting to new challenges.

Invest in Professional Development

Make a commitment to invest in your professional development by taking courses, attending workshops, or earning certifications related to your side hustle. Whether it's learning new marketing strategies, mastering a software tool, or developing leadership skills, continuous learning helps you stay relevant and improve your business.

Many online platforms, such as Coursera, Udemy, and LinkedIn Learning, offer courses on a wide range of topics, allowing you to learn at your own pace. Consider setting aside time each month to focus on learning something new that can benefit your side hustle.

Encourage Team Development

If you have a team, it's important to invest in their development as well. Encourage your employees or freelancers to pursue learning opportunities that align with their roles and contribute to your business's growth. This could include attending industry conferences, enrolling in online courses, or participating in skill-building workshops.

Provide access to resources, mentorship, and training programs that support your team's growth. A culture of continuous learning not only enhances your team's capabilities but also fosters innovation and creativity within your business.

Stay Open to New Ideas

Innovation often comes from being open to new ideas and perspectives. Surround yourself with diverse voices, whether through networking, mentorship, or collaboration, to gain fresh insights and challenge your thinking.

Join entrepreneurial communities, mastermind groups, or industry forums where you can exchange ideas with others and learn from their experiences. Being open to new ideas helps you stay adaptable and discover new ways to grow your side hustle.

Embrace a Growth Mindset

A growth mindset—the belief that your abilities and intelligence can be developed through effort, learning, and persistence—is key to continuous learning and development. Embrace challenges as opportunities to grow, and view setbacks as valuable lessons rather than failures.

Encourage a growth mindset within your team by celebrating efforts, learning from mistakes, and fostering a culture of curiosity and experimentation. By adopting a growth mindset, you'll be better equipped to navigate change and continuously improve your side hustle.

Preparing for Long-Term Success

To ensure the long-term success of your side hustle, it's important to plan for the future and build a strong foundation for sustainable growth. This involves setting clear goals, maintaining financial health, and building a brand that can withstand the test of time.

Set Long-Term Goals

While short-term goals help you achieve immediate milestones, long-term goals provide a vision for where you want your side hustle to be in the future. Consider where you want your business to be in five, ten, or even twenty years. What are your ultimate aspirations? Do you want to scale to a full-time business, expand into new markets, or create a legacy brand?

Set clear, measurable long-term goals that align with your vision and break them down into actionable steps. Regularly review and adjust your goals as needed to ensure they remain relevant and achievable as your business evolves.

Maintain Financial Health

Financial stability is crucial for the long-term success of your side hustle. To ensure your business remains financially healthy, regularly monitor your cash flow, manage expenses, and build an emergency fund to cover unexpected challenges.

Create a financial plan that includes budgeting, forecasting, and setting aside savings for future investments or expansion. Consider working with an accountant or financial advisor to help you manage your finances effectively and make informed decisions.

Build a Strong Brand

A strong brand is an invaluable asset that can help you weather changes in the market and build lasting relationships with customers. Focus on building a brand that resonates with your target audience, reflects your values, and stands out in your industry.

Consistently deliver on your brand promise by providing high-quality products or services, exceptional customer experiences, and authentic communication. Over time, a strong brand can become synonymous with trust, reliability, and value, helping you retain customers and attract new ones.

Focus on Customer Loyalty

Customer loyalty is key to sustaining long-term success. Happy, loyal customers are more likely to make repeat purchases, refer others, and become brand advocates. To build customer loyalty, prioritize exceptional customer service, engage with your audience regularly, and reward loyalty through special offers, discounts, or loyalty programs.

Gather feedback from your customers and use it to continuously improve your products, services, and customer experiences. By focusing on customer satisfaction and building strong relationships, you can create a loyal customer base that supports your side hustle for years to come.

Prepare for Succession and Exit Planning

Even if you're not planning to sell your side hustle or step down anytime soon, it's wise to think about succession and exit planning. This involves preparing your business for the possibility of a leadership transition, sale, or merger.

Consider what steps you would need to take to make your business attractive to potential buyers or successors. This could include documenting your processes, building a strong management team, and ensuring financial transparency. Succession and exit planning provide peace of mind and ensure that your business can continue to thrive, even if you're no longer at the helm.

Adapt to Change with Agility

The ability to adapt to change with agility is perhaps the most important aspect of future-proofing your business. Markets, technologies, and consumer preferences will continue to evolve, and the most successful businesses are those that can pivot quickly and effectively.

Stay flexible, be willing to experiment, and embrace change as an opportunity for growth. By cultivating an agile mindset and approach, you'll be better prepared to navigate whatever challenges or opportunities the future may bring.

Future-proofing your side hustle is about building a business that can withstand the test of time, adapt to changes, and continue to grow and thrive. By staying informed, continuously learning, and planning for the long term, you can set your side hustle on a path to sustainable success. The entrepreneurial journey is filled with both challenges and opportunities, but with the right strategies in place, you can build a business that not only survives but flourishes in the years to come.

Conclusion

As you reach the end of this guide, it's time to reflect on the journey you've embarked upon with your side hustle. You've learned how to turn an idea into reality, navigate the challenges of entrepreneurship, and lay the foundation for long-term success. But this is only the beginning. Your side hustle has the potential to grow and evolve into something truly remarkable, and with the right mindset and strategies, you can continue to build on everything you've achieved so far.

Reflecting on Your Journey

Starting a side hustle is no small feat. It takes courage, determination, and a willingness to step outside of your comfort zone. Reflect on the journey you've taken—how far you've come since you first had the idea, the challenges you've overcome, and the successes you've celebrated along the way.

Think about the lessons you've learned, the skills you've developed, and the personal growth you've experienced. Whether you've launched your first product, gained your first customer, or reached a significant milestone, each achievement is a testament to your hard work and perseverance.

This journey has likely had its share of ups and downs, but every experience, whether positive or negative, has contributed to your growth as an entrepreneur. Take pride in how much you've accomplished and use this reflection as a source of motivation as you move forward.

Next Steps and Growth Opportunities

While you've already made significant progress, there are always new opportunities to explore and goals to achieve. Consider what the next steps are for your side hustle. What areas do you want to focus on in the coming months or years? How can you continue to grow and evolve your business?

- **Scaling Your Business:** If you haven't already, think about how you can scale your side hustle to reach a larger audience, increase revenue, or expand your product or service offerings. Scaling might involve automating processes, hiring help, or entering new markets.
- **Expanding Your Skillset:** Continuous learning is key to staying competitive and driving growth. Identify areas where you can improve your skills, whether it's in marketing, finance, leadership, or product development. Investing in your education will pay dividends as you continue to grow your business.
- **Exploring New Markets:** Are there untapped markets or customer segments that could benefit from your products or services? Consider how you can expand your reach by targeting new audiences, offering new products, or entering international markets.
- **Building Stronger Relationships:** Strengthen the relationships you've built with your customers, partners, and community. Loyal customers and supportive networks are invaluable assets that can drive referrals, collaborations, and long-term success.
- **Setting New Goals:** As you reflect on your journey, set new goals that align with your vision for the future. These goals should be specific, measurable, and ambitious enough to challenge you to continue growing and innovating.

Encouragement to Keep Going

The road of entrepreneurship is often challenging, but it's also incredibly rewarding. There will be times when you face setbacks, experience self-doubt, or feel overwhelmed by the demands of running a side hustle. During these moments, it's important to remember why you started in the first place.

Your side hustle is more than just a business—it's a reflection of your passions, your creativity, and your drive to make a difference. The progress you've made so far is proof that you have what it takes to succeed. Keep that in mind whenever you encounter obstacles.

Stay committed to your vision, and don't be afraid to take risks, experiment, and learn from your experiences. Surround yourself with supportive people who believe in you and your mission. Celebrate your successes, no matter how small, and use them as fuel to keep pushing forward.

Remember, success doesn't happen overnight. It's the result of consistent effort, resilience, and a willingness to adapt and grow. The journey may be long, but the rewards are worth it. Every step you take brings you closer to your goals, and with each challenge you overcome, you become a stronger and more capable entrepreneur.

So, keep going. The future of your side hustle is full of potential, and with the knowledge, skills, and determination you've gained, there's no limit to what you can achieve. The world needs your unique ideas, your creativity, and your drive—so continue to build, create, and make your mark.

You've already accomplished so much, and the best is yet to come. Here's to your ongoing success, growth, and the exciting journey ahead.

Resources

Building and growing a successful side hustle requires the right tools, knowledge, and support. This section provides a curated list of resources, including templates, tools, recommended reading, and online courses and communities, to help you on your entrepreneurial journey.

Templates, Tools, and Worksheets

Business Plan Template: A well-structured business plan is essential for outlining your goals, strategies, and financial projections. Use this template to create a comprehensive business plan that will guide your side hustle's growth.

-

    Download: Business Plan Template

Budgeting and Financial Planning Worksheet: Effective budgeting and financial planning are critical for managing your side hustle's finances. This worksheet helps you track income, expenses, and cash flow to ensure financial stability.

-

    Download: Budgeting and Financial Planning Worksheet

Marketing Strategy Template: A clear marketing strategy is key to attracting customers and growing your side hustle. This template guides you through the process of defining your target audience, setting goals, and choosing the right marketing channels.

-

    Download: Marketing Strategy Template

Social Media Content Calendar: Consistency is crucial for building an online presence. Use this content calendar template to plan and schedule your social media posts, ensuring you stay engaged with your audience.

-

    Download: Social Media Content Calendar

Task Management Checklist: Staying organized is essential when juggling multiple responsibilities. This checklist helps you prioritize tasks, set deadlines, and track progress to maximize productivity.

-

    Download: Task Management Checklist

Customer Feedback Survey: Understanding your customers' needs and preferences is vital for improving your products or services. Use this survey template to gather valuable feedback and insights from your customers.

-

    Download: Customer Feedback Survey

Goal-Setting Worksheet: Setting and tracking goals is important for measuring your progress and staying motivated. This worksheet helps you define SMART goals and break them down into actionable steps.

-

    Download: Goal-Setting Worksheet

Recommended Reading

1. *The Lean Startup* by Eric Ries This book introduces the Lean Startup methodology, which emphasizes rapid experimentation and iterative product development. It's a must-read for anyone looking to build a side hustle that can adapt quickly to market changes.

2. *Atomic Habits* by James Clear James Clear's book on habit formation is perfect for entrepreneurs looking to build productive routines and make lasting changes. Learn how small habits can lead to significant improvements in both your personal and professional life.

3. *Crushing It!* by Gary Vaynerchuk Gary Vaynerchuk shares inspiring stories of entrepreneurs who have turned their passions into profitable businesses. This book offers practical advice on how to build your personal brand and leverage social media for success.

4. *Profit First* by Mike Michalowicz Managing finances is crucial for any side hustle. In *Profit First*, Mike Michalowicz introduces a unique cash management system that ensures your business is profitable from day one.

5. *The $100 Startup* by Chris Guillebeau Chris Guillebeau's book is a great resource for anyone looking to start a business on a tight budget. It's filled with case studies of successful entrepreneurs who started with minimal investment and scaled their businesses.

6. *Deep Work* by Cal Newport *Deep Work* explores the importance of focused, uninterrupted work in achieving significant results. This book is particularly useful for side hustlers who need to maximize productivity in limited time.

7. *Start with Why* by Simon Sinek Simon Sinek's book delves into the power of understanding your purpose and how it can drive success in your business. It's a great read for entrepreneurs looking to build a brand that resonates with their audience.

Online Courses and Communities

1. Coursera: Entrepreneurship Specializations Coursera offers a variety of entrepreneurship courses and specializations from top universities. Topics range from business planning and marketing to financial management and innovation. These courses are perfect for side hustlers looking to build their skills.

-

    Visit:Coursera Entrepreneurship Courses

2. Udemy: Small Business and Side Hustle Courses Udemy provides a wide range of affordable courses on topics like starting a side hustle, digital marketing, e-commerce, and more. Courses are taught by industry experts and come with lifetime access.

-

    Visit:Udemy Side Hustle Courses

3. Skillshare: Creative and Business Skills Skillshare offers thousands of classes on creative skills, entrepreneurship, and business development. It's an excellent platform for side hustlers looking to learn new skills, from graphic design to productivity hacks.

-

    Visit:Skillshare

4. LinkedIn Learning: Business and Professional Development LinkedIn Learning provides access to a vast library of courses on business, technology, and creative skills. It's a great resource for side hustlers looking to enhance their professional development.

-

    Visit:LinkedIn Learning

5. The Side Hustle School Podcast by Chris Guillebeau This daily podcast features stories of people who have successfully started side hustles, offering practical advice and inspiration. It's a great way to stay motivated and learn from others who have walked the same path.

- **Visit:** Side Hustle School Podcast

6. Reddit: r/Entrepreneur and r/SideHustle Reddit's entrepreneur and side hustle communities are excellent places to connect with fellow entrepreneurs, ask questions, share experiences, and get advice. These communities are active and supportive, making them great resources for ongoing learning and networking.

- **Visit:** r/Entrepreneur |r/SideHustle

7. The Entrepreneurs' Organization (EO) EO is a global network of entrepreneurs who support each other through networking events, mentorship, and educational resources. It's an excellent community for those looking to take their side hustle to the next level.

- **Visit:** Entrepreneurs' Organization

8. The Freelancers Union The Freelancers Union offers resources, benefits, and a community for freelancers and side hustlers. They provide valuable information on legal issues, health insurance, and financial planning for independent workers.

- **Visit:** Freelancers Union

These resources are designed to support you at every stage of your side hustle journey, from planning and launching to scaling and sustaining success. By leveraging these tools, reading materials, and learning opportunities, you can continue to grow your business, develop new skills, and stay connected with a community of like-minded entrepreneurs. Remember, the key to long-term success is continuous learning and adaptation—so keep exploring, experimenting, and evolving as you build your side hustle into something extraordinary.

Appendix

Glossary of Terms

Understanding key business terms is essential for navigating the world of entrepreneurship. This glossary provides definitions for important terms you'll encounter as you build and grow your side hustle.

1. Break-Even Point:
The point at which total revenue equals total costs, meaning the business is neither making a profit nor a loss. It's the minimum level of sales needed to cover expenses.

2. Business Plan:
A formal document that outlines your business goals, strategies, target market, and financial projections. It serves as a roadmap for your business's growth and development.

3. Cash Flow:
The movement of money in and out of your business. Positive cash flow means you have more money coming in than going out, while negative cash flow indicates the opposite.

4. Competitive Analysis:
The process of identifying and evaluating your competitors' strengths and weaknesses to inform your own business strategy.

5. Customer Acquisition Cost (CAC):
The cost associated with acquiring a new customer, including marketing and sales expenses. It's calculated by dividing total acquisition costs by the number of new customers gained.

6. Customer Relationship Management (CRM):
A system or software used to manage and analyze customer interactions and data throughout the customer lifecycle, with the goal of improving customer relationships and driving sales growth.

7. E-commerce:
The buying and selling of goods or services over the internet. E-commerce businesses can operate entirely online or as part of a larger brick-and-mortar operation.

8. Freelancing:
Offering services to clients on a project or contract basis, rather than being employed full-time by a single employer. Freelancers often work independently and manage multiple clients simultaneously.

9. Gross Profit:
The difference between total revenue and the cost of goods sold (COGS). It represents the profit made from selling products or services before deducting operating expenses.

10. Market Research:
The process of gathering, analyzing, and interpreting information about a market, including information about potential customers, competitors, and industry trends.

11. Minimum Viable Product (MVP):
A product with just enough features to satisfy early customers and provide feedback for future development. The MVP approach allows businesses to test concepts and iterate quickly.

12. Niche Market:
A specific, well-defined segment of a larger market that has its own unique needs, preferences, and demands. Businesses often focus on niche markets to target a more specific audience.

13. Pay-Per-Click (PPC):
An online advertising model in which advertisers pay each time a user clicks on one of their ads. It's commonly used in search engine and social media advertising.

14. Return on Investment (ROI):
A measure of the profitability of an investment, calculated by

dividing the net profit by the initial investment cost. ROI is often expressed as a percentage.

15. Search Engine Optimization (SEO):
The practice of optimizing a website or content to rank higher in search engine results, with the goal of increasing organic (unpaid) traffic.

16. Social Proof:
The influence that the actions, behaviors, or opinions of others have on an individual's decision-making process. Social proof can include customer testimonials, reviews, endorsements, and social media mentions.

17. Target Audience:
The specific group of people a business aims to reach with its products, services, and marketing efforts. Understanding the target audience is crucial for effective marketing and product development.

18. Value Proposition:
A statement that clearly communicates the unique benefits and value a product or service offers to customers, explaining why they should choose it over competitors.

19. Venture Capital:
A form of private equity financing provided by investors to startups and small businesses with high growth potential. Venture capitalists typically take an equity stake in the company in exchange for funding.

20. Workflow Automation:
The use of technology to automate repetitive tasks and processes, allowing businesses to operate more efficiently and focus on higher-value activities.

Additional Case Studies and Examples

Case Study 1: The Local Artisanal Food Brand

Background: Mark, a full-time software engineer with a passion for cooking, started experimenting with making artisanal sauces and spreads in his kitchen. Friends and family loved his creations, encouraging him to sell them at local farmers' markets. What began as a small weekend project quickly gained traction as more people discovered his unique flavors.

Challenges: Mark faced the challenge of scaling production while maintaining the quality of his handmade products. Additionally, he needed to navigate the complexities of food regulations and labeling requirements. Balancing his demanding job with the increasing demands of his side hustle also proved challenging.

Strategies:

- **Local Partnerships:** Mark partnered with local farms to source fresh, organic ingredients, which not only supported local agriculture but also differentiated his brand as a farm-to-table product.
- **Online Sales:** He set up an e-commerce website to reach customers beyond his local market, allowing him to sell his products nationwide. He used social media to drive traffic to his site and promote special offers.
- **Product Line Expansion:** After successfully launching his first line of sauces, Mark expanded his offerings to include spreads, dressings, and marinades, appealing to a wider range of customers.

Results: Mark's side hustle grew into a well-known local brand with a loyal customer base. He eventually transitioned to working on his business full-time, secured a spot on the shelves of local grocery stores, and even won several awards for his products.

Lessons Learned:

- **Quality Consistency:** Maintaining product quality while scaling production is crucial for building and retaining customer loyalty.

- **Regulatory Compliance:** Understanding and adhering to industry regulations, especially in food production, is essential for avoiding legal issues and ensuring customer safety.

- **Community Engagement:** Building strong relationships with local partners and customers can create a supportive community that helps your business thrive.

Case Study 2: The Digital Marketing Consultant

Background: Lena was a full-time marketing manager who noticed a growing demand for digital marketing expertise among small businesses in her community. With years of experience in the corporate world, she decided to start a side hustle offering digital marketing consulting services. Her goal was to help small businesses improve their online presence and reach their target audience more effectively.

Challenges: Lena's main challenges included building a client base from scratch, managing multiple clients while working full-time, and staying up-to-date with the ever-changing landscape of digital marketing tools and strategies.

Strategies:

-

- **Niche Focus:** Lena focused on serving small businesses in specific industries, such as local retail and hospitality, where she had deep knowledge and could provide tailored solutions.
- **Content Marketing:** She started a blog and a LinkedIn newsletter where she shared digital marketing tips, case studies, and industry insights. This content helped establish her as an expert in her niche and attracted potential clients.
- **Networking:** Lena attended local business events, joined networking groups, and leveraged her existing connections to find clients. She offered free initial consultations to build trust and showcase her expertise.

Results: Lena's side hustle quickly gained traction, and within a year, she had a steady stream of clients. She was able to increase her rates as her reputation grew and eventually left her full-time job to focus on her consulting business. Lena also expanded her services to include online courses and workshops, creating additional revenue streams.

Lessons Learned:

- **Specialization:** Focusing on a specific niche allowed Lena to differentiate herself and offer more value to her clients.
- **Thought Leadership:** Consistently sharing valuable content helped Lena build her personal brand and attract clients organically.
- **Client Relationships:** Building strong, trust-based relationships with clients is key to securing repeat business and referrals.

Case Study 3: The Freelance Graphic Designer

Background: Carlos was a graphic designer working at a design agency but wanted more creative freedom and the ability to choose his projects. He decided to start freelancing on the side, offering design services to startups and small businesses. His goal was to build a portfolio of diverse work and eventually transition to freelancing full-time.

Challenges: Carlos faced challenges in finding clients, setting his rates, and managing multiple projects simultaneously. Additionally, balancing his agency job with freelance work required careful time management and organization.

Strategies:

- **Portfolio Development:** Carlos created an online portfolio showcasing his best work, including personal projects that demonstrated his skills in different design styles. This helped him attract clients who were looking for a specific aesthetic.
- **Freelance Platforms:** He signed up for freelance platforms like Upwork and Fiverr to find clients and build his reputation. He started with smaller projects to gain experience and positive reviews.
- **Time Management:** Carlos used time-blocking techniques to allocate specific hours to his freelance work, ensuring that he met deadlines without compromising his full-time job performance.

Results: Carlos's freelance business grew steadily, and within two years, he had enough clients to leave his agency job and freelance full-time. He built a strong reputation for delivering high-quality work on time and was able to raise his rates and attract larger clients.

Lessons Learned:

- **Portfolio Importance:** A well-curated portfolio is essential for showcasing your skills and attracting the right clients.
- **Start Small:** Building a freelance business takes time, and starting with smaller projects can help you gain experience, build a reputation, and grow your client base.
- **Time Management:** Effective time management is crucial for balancing a full-time job with freelancing and ensuring consistent quality in your work.

These additional case studies highlight the diverse paths entrepreneurs take to build successful side hustles. Whether you're starting with a physical product, offering a service, or freelancing, the key lessons from these examples can guide you in overcoming challenges, seizing opportunities, and achieving your goals. Each journey is unique, but the common thread is a commitment to learning, adapting, and persevering in the face of obstacles. By applying these insights to your own side hustle, you can continue to grow and succeed on your entrepreneurial journey.

www.ingramcontent.com/pod-product-compliance
Lightning Source LLC
Chambersburg PA
CBHW071100240526
45471CB00016B/2204